Saints in Herefordshire

Saints in Herefordshire
A Study of Dedications

by

D.M. Annett

D.M. Annett
in association with
Logaston Press

LOGASTON PRESS
Little Logaston, Logaston,
Woonton, Almeley, Herefordshire HR3 6QH

First published by D.M. Annett & Logaston Press 1999
Copyright text © The Herefordshire Historic Churches Trust 1999
Illustrations of stained glass © Joe Hillaby 1999

All rights reserved. No part of this publication
may be reproduced, stored in a retrieval system,
or transmitted, in any form or by any means,
electronic, mechanical, photocopying, recording
or otherwise, without the prior permission,
in writing of the publisher

ISBN 1 873827 26 1

Set in Times by Logaston Press
and printed in Great Britain by
The Cromwell Press, Trowbridge

Cover illustration: St George; Brinsop

Contents

	page
Acknowledgements	vii
Notes on the Illustrations	viii
The Herefordshire Historic Churches Trust	ix
Preface	xi
The Dedication of Churches	1
The Patron Saints	9
References	37
List A. Alphabetical List of Dedications by Patron Saints	39
List B. Alphabetical List of Dedications by Parishes	43
Appendix I Changes of Dedication	51
Appendix II Charters for Parochial Fairs	61
Appendix III Inabwy/Junabius	63
References to Appendices	65
Bibliography	67

ACKNOWLEDGEMENTS

As an amateur plunged unexpectedly into research, I should have been lost but for the guidance and help of Mr Bruce Coplestone Crow and Mrs Phyllis Williams, who generously gave me the benefit of their wide-ranging knowledge. Miss S. Hubbard at the Hereford Record Office and Miss J. Williams at the Cathedral Library have dealt helpfully and patiently with my many queries. Mrs Muriel Tonkin has kindly kept a look-out for dedications while indexing the pre-Reformation wills in the County Record Office but, surprisingly, no relevant material has yet come to light. My son-in-law Allan Wyatt and my brother John have given much editorial and clerical assistance. I am very grateful to them all, and to many other correspondents who have supplied information. I am also indebted to the Dean and Chapter of Hereford Cathedral for allowing use of the illustration of the brass of St Ethelbert. Most of all am I indebted to my friend and mentor Joe Hillaby, without whose constant guidance, help and encouragement over several years this study would never have seen the light of day. As a final benefaction he has provided all the illustrations of the stained glass. It is no exaggeration to say that almost anything of value in the following pages is his, while any deficiencies and errors are mine.

NOTES ON THE ILLUSTRATIONS

Brinsop:	In the east window are two early 14th-century panels one of which shows St George, to whom the church is dedicated.
Credenhill;	The south chancel window contains a beautiful small panel of early 14th-century glass representing St Thomas of Canterbury (Becket) and St Thomas of Hereford (Cantilupe).
Dore Abbey;	The east window is filled with glass dated 1634, being part of Lord Scudamore's restoration of the church.
Eaton Bishop:	The east and south-east windows in the chancel contain very fine glass dating from about 1330.
Hereford:	The brass of St Ethelbert was one of two smaller brasses either side of one of St Thomas Cantilupe affixed to the base of the latter's shrine. It was made by 1287 by the Ashford workshop in London and is believed to be one of the earliest English brasses.
Ludlow:	The great east window contains 27 scenes from the life of St Laurence, to whom the church is dedicated. The glass originally dates from the 15th-century, but was heavily restored in the 19th century. The same applies to the figure of St Catherine from a side window.
Old Radnor:	This fine church, though in Wales, is in the diocese of Hereford. It has some fragments of old glass, including a late 15th-century figure of St Catherine.
Ross-on-Wye:	In the east window are three figures of 15th-century glass. These were removed from the house of the bishops of Hereford at Stretton Sugwas when this was dismantled in 1792.
Sellack;	The east window is filled with glass dated 1630, though it contains some other fragments.

THE HEREFORDSHIRE HISTORIC CHURCHES TRUST

All profits from the sale of this book will be given to the Herefordshire Historic Churches Trust. The Trust was founded in 1954 to raise money for the maintenance, repair and restoration of the historic churches and chapels of Herefordshire. In the county there are 325 Anglican churches in regular use, most of them mediæval at least in part, and in addition a large number of churches and chapels of other Christian bodies—Roman Catholic, Methodist etc.—which fall within the Trust's remit. It is sometimes thought that parish churches are maintained by the Church Commissioners, the diocese or the state, but this is not so: the full responsibility falls on the individual parish. In a rural county like Herefordshire many of the churches are remote and the congregations small, so the upkeep of the building can pose serious financial problems, particularly when urgent and expensive repairs are needed. In such cases a grant or loan from the Trust can come as a great help and encouragement.

The Trust is supported entirely by voluntary subscriptions, donations and legacies. In the five years from 1994 to 1998, 85 churches and chapels were assisted with grants or loans totalling over £200,000. Information about the Trust can be obtained from the Secretary, The Herefordshire Historic Churches Trust, The Palace, Hereford HR4 9BL.

PREFACE

The original intention of this study was to provide lists of the dedications of Herefordshire churches and brief notes on their patron saints. As I proceeded, I found to my surprise that many of the churches had had their dedications changed at some time, but that it was—also to my surprise—difficult in many cases to find evidence for the date of the change. Such evidence usually appears only in chance references in the Bishops' Registers, in wills and in other records. In order to keep the main body of the text as free as possible from footnotes and references, I have relegated the details of changed and variant dedications to Appendix I. (Since Junabius turned out to be a controversial figure, I have given him an Appendix of his own.)

A word should be said about the *Book of Llandaff*, to which frequent reference is made in the following pages. This is a 12th-century collection comprising chiefly a series of charters dating back to the 6th century, and containing also 'lives' of several local saints, including Dyfrig and Clydog. The charters, which have been closely studied by Wendy Davies in her book *The Llandaff Charters* (1979) give much information about religious foundations in Archenfield (Ergyng), which was administered from Llandaff before being incorporated into the diocese of Hereford. References are to *The Text of the Book of Llan Dav* (ed. J.G. Evans) published in 1893 and reprinted in facsimile by the National Library of Wales in 1979.

Finally, recognition must be made of the dazzling new light which was thrown on the whole subject by the publication in 1996 of Professor Nicholas Orme's book *English Church Dedications—with a Survey of Cornwall and Devon*. An extremely comprehensive and illuminating introduction to the whole subject of dedications is followed by gazetteers of the two counties. These cover all mediaeval religious houses and ancient (*i.e.* pre-1800) parish churches, and each entry consists of three parts; the first gives all documentary references to the patron saint in chronological order, the second collects evidence about dedication festivals and parish feasts, and the third gives an editorial commentary on this evidence. All this research demonstrates strikingly that many apparent 'changes' were in fact mistaken attempts by 18th-century antiquaries to discover lost mediæval dedications. I shall return to this point later. Orme's book is obviously a landmark in the study of dedications, and sets a pattern to be followed in other counties. This present modest exercise may perhaps serve as a stimulus to some properly qualified historian to do for Herefordshire what Orme has so admirably done for Cornwall and Devon. Meanwhile I shall be grateful for any additional information about what for convenience I shall still refer to as 'changes', and of course for any corrections.

D.M.A.
Newland 1999

THE DEDICATION OF CHURCHES

Strictly speaking 'dedication' involves a declaration that the church is devoted to sacred purposes, while 'consecration' is the liturgical action making the place holy. All churches are therefore dedicated to God, but from early times it became usual to place a church under a particular patron, after whom the church might be named. From this the term 'dedication' came to be generally but inaccurately used to apply to the dedication of a patron—usually a saint, but sometimes an aspect of the Deity (*e.g.* Christ Church, the Holy Trinity) or an incident in Christ's life (*e.g.* the Ascension, the Nativity). The ceremony of dedication had to be performed by the diocesan bishop. (In 1229 Bishop William of Blois required that in all the churches in his diocese of Worcester there should be displayed the date of their dedication, the name of the officiating bishop, and the patron saint. If such records had survived, the lot of the researcher would have been much easier.)

Anyone studying the dedications of Herefordshire churches will soon be made aware of two significant historical features. The first, which Herefordshire shares only with Cornwall among the English counties, is the influence of the Celtic Church in the south and west parts of the county—the old kingdoms of Ergyng (Archenfield) and Ewyas. Here dedications commemorate the surprisingly peripatetic saints more usually associated with North Wales, such as Beuno, Deiniol (Deinst) and Tysilio, as well as truly local figures such as Dyfrig, Inabwy and Cynidr. The three 'martyred' princes, Alkmund, Clydog and Ethelbert, add a further colourful element. It is regrettable that St Thomas of Hereford (Thomas Cantilupe) has no Anglican dedications in his own county, though his namesake of Canterbury has two.

The second feature is that the county was almost untouched by the Industrial Revolution of the 19th century, so there was no sudden increase of population needing ecclesiastical provision. In Hereford city four churches were built in the 19th and two in the 20th century to serve the new suburbs (and one of the former, St Martin's, is a refoundation on a new site of a destroyed mediæval church), but none of the five market towns has outgrown its mediaeval parish church. A few new churches were built to serve expanded residential areas such as Upper Colwall and Wellington Heath, but the great majority of churches in the county are mediaeval foundations, with a remarkable number still showing architectural evidence of their origins in the 12th century or even earlier.

The first saints were martyrs. The dates of their deaths were recorded in martyrologies—the earliest church calendars—and churches were usually built over the place of their martyrdom, containing a shrine which held the relics of the saint. These became places of pilgrimage, or at least focal points for local cults. The churches were called *memoriae* or *martyria*, and this usage survives in some Welsh place-names; Merthyr Tydfil marks the burial place of St Tydfil, while Clodock in Herefordshire, the final resting-place of the body of the murdered Prince Clydog, appears in an 8th-century charter as *Merthirclitauc*.[1]

Later, but still in early times, two other classes of saints were added—confessors and virgins (who were often also martyrs). These had borne notable witness to the Faith by their lives, and their sanctity was attested by miracles both before and after death. These too, where possible, had churches with shrines built over the places of their death. These shrines are not uncommon in cathedrals and monastic churches, as for example those of Edward the Confessor in Westminster Abbey and of Alban the Martyr in St Alban's Abbey, but they are rare in parish churches. Two remarkable survivals are at Whitchurch Canonicorum in Dorset, where the shrine of St Wite (Candida) remains almost intact, and at Pennant Melangell in Powys, where the shrine of St Melangell (Monacella) has recently been restored.

At the consecration of a new church, provision was made during the ceremonial for the enclosing of relics in the structure of the high altar. If no relics of a local saint were available, any other venerable relics were acceptable, and these were often given by benefactors. (The small stone structure in the church of SS. Cosmas and Damian at Stretford in Herefordshire is described as a shrine, and did indeed contain relics, for offerings were made at it until the Reformation (see p.14), but they can hardly have been relics of the patron saints, which would have been enclosed in the high altar.)

Originally the title of 'saint' was given by popular acclaim; later however certification of sainthood by a bishop was considered necessary, and finally, from the 13th century, this authority was reserved to the Pope. Over the centuries an elaborate and protracted procedure was developed for investigating the life and miracles of candidates, leading first to the award of the title Blessed (Beatification) and ultimately to that of Saint (Canonisation). This procedure was codified by Pope Benedict XIV in about 1750 and, with modifications, is followed today in the Roman Church. No similar procedure exists in the Anglican Church, which has created no new saints since the Reformation, though several more recent figures are commemorated in the latest version of the Church Calendar.

In the Celtic Church the title of saint was given much more freely. and many Celtic 'saints' were merely missioners who were the first to evangelise an area. Celtic churches were consecrated but not dedicated, and often bear the name of their founder, who later acquired the 'courtesy title' of patron saint.

Dedications may be divided into four classes: (i) some aspect of the Deity; (ii) scriptural saints; (iii) legendary saints; and (iv) native saints. The numbers of churches in the county bearing each dedication are given in brackets.

The Virgin and Child; Eaton Bishop

(i) The Deity

Under this heading can be placed Christ Church (3), the Holy Trinity (6), the Holy Rood (1) and the Good Shepherd (1). The total numbers may seem surprisingly small, but it must be remembered, as Francis Bond points out, that strictly speaking 'every church is dedicated to God in memory of such and such a saint or event.'[2]

(ii) Scriptural Saints

Only a few of these have their full life and death recorded in the Gospels and the Acts, for example John the Baptist and Stephen. Almost all the others are subject to legendary extensions of their life-stories, often culminating in martyrdom, *e.g.* Andrew, Peter and Paul. (Michael is in a class by himself, having had no earthly life.) In this category the most popular are the Blessed Virgin Mary (50), Michael (32), John the Baptist (24) and Peter (20).

(iii) Legendary Saints
These may have a basis of historical fact (though even this is doubtful in the case of Catherine of Alexandria and Margaret of Antioch, for example), but this has usually been overlaid by a mass of highly imaginative and often contradictory legends, derived from 'Acts' or 'Lives' of the saints often written some centuries after the death of the subject, and owing more to pious fiction than historical fact. It is astonishing that so many of these shadowy and implausible figures became such popular and venerated saints in mediaeval times. Even that serious and scholarly authority Miss F. Arnold-Forster is driven to surmise that 'mediaeval founders esteemed a saint in direct proportion to the number of incredible stories told about him or her.'[3] Examples of this category are Giles (6), Lawrence (5), George (4) and Margaret (3).

(iv) Native Saints
This class consists chiefly of Celtic missioners such as Dyfrig/Dubricius (8) and Dewi/David (4), although it can be stretched to include three figures from further afield, Alkmund (1), Ethelbert (1) and Thomas of Canterbury (2). It has already been noted that the title to 'sainthood' of some of the former is rather tenuous, while the award of the martyr's crown to such figures as Alkmund, Clydog and Ethelbert is equally questionable. They may well have been Christian princes of exemplary life who met a violent end, but they can hardly be said to have died for their faith, since their deaths were due rather to reasons of passion or politics. (Henry VIII held the same view of Thomas à Becket, though he would not have conceded even the 'exemplary life'.)

Choice of Dedication
There are many possible reasons for the original choice of a dedication. The chosen saint may have been the personal patron of the lord of the manor or of the bishop who consecrated the church, or of the monastery to which the church was appropriated. The dedication may commemorate the founder of the church (*e.g.* Beuno at Llanveynoe) or the death or burial place of a local saint (*e.g.* Clydog at Clodock and Ethelbert at Hereford). The choice may be due to the current popularity of the cult of a particular saint (*e.g.* Margaret or Bartholomew). In the 18th century new town churches were often dedicated to St Anne or St George as a compliment to the reigning monarch. In the 19th and 20th centuries many of the new churches were dedicated to previously unpopular scriptural saints such as Matthew, Matthias and Barnabas—and, most notably, Paul. These last two categories are hardly represented in Herefordshire since, except for the six churches in the suburbs of Hereford, there have been few new foundations since the 13th century.

DEDICATION OF CHURCHES

Changes of Dedication

When a church was originally dedicated to a 'native' saint, the dedication may have been changed by the addition or substitution of a more respectable scriptural saint. Examples of the former are Aymestrey (John Baptist added to Alkmund) and Llanveynoe (Peter added to Beuno), and of the latter Kentchurch (Mary superseding Keyne) and Llanwarne (John Baptist superseding Dyfrig and Teilo). There are various periods and occasions when these changes are most likely to have occurred.

(i) After the Conquest the Normans, partly for political reasons, tried to abolish or at least diminish the cults of the 'native' saints. The campaign was led by Lanfranc, the first Norman Archbishop of Canterbury, who had a poor opinion of the credentials of most Celtic and Anglo-Saxon saints. (At Evesham Abbey the first Norman abbot, Walter, doubting the sanctity of the two Saxon saints Credan and Wistan, subjected their relics to ordeal by fire—but they stood the test.)

St Barnabas;
Eaton Bishop

(ii) When a church was rebuilt or significantly enlarged it was often reconsecrated, and the officiating bishop sometimes took the opportunity to rededicate the church—in some cases to his personal patron saint.

(iii) In the 13th and 14th centuries the cult of the Blessed Virgin Mary was at its height, and many churches were rededicated to her.

(iv) In the 14th and 15th centuries obscure local saints were sometimes replaced by popular favourites such as Lawrence, Giles and Bartholomew.

(v) What appears to be a change of dedication can in fact most frequently be explained by the suppression of the cult of the saints at the Reformation, followed 150 years later by the well-meaning but often misguided attempts of 18th-century antiquaries to recover lost mediaeval dedications. How this occurred must be explained more fully.

Until the Reformation each parish celebrated two particular feast-days— the festival of the patron saint of the church as given in the Church Calendar (the Patronal Festival), and the anniversary of the act of dedication of the church by the bishop (the Dedication Festival). These holy days were holidays, and of course varied from parish to parish, thereby causing much interruption to work and great vexation to Reformers and Puritans. In 1536 Henry VIII ordered all churches to keep their Dedication Festivals on the first Sunday in October, while the Patronal Festival was no longer to be observed as a public holiday. This was part of the Reformers' campaign to eliminate the cults of the saints, which were regarded as superstitious, and with the removal of the two parish holidays (but see below for the continuation of the parish feasts) remembrance of the patron saints was weakened over the years, and in many cases entirely forgotten. This was of course the aim of the Reformers, and it was reinforced by the removal or destruction of images in churches, as was ordered in 1548.

For the next century and a half, therefore, the name of the patron saint to whom each church was dedicated vanished in many cases both from folk-memory and from documentary records, and it was not until the early 18th century that antiquaries began to take an interest in the ancient dedications, and to try to recover them. The first of these was Browne Willis (1682-1760) who in 1727-1733 published diocesan lists of parish churches with all the dedications which he thought he had recovered. This material was revised and re-issued by John Ecton in 1742 under the title *Thesaurus Rerum Ecclesiasticarum*. Willis's researches into mediaeval documents were frustrated, as are modern researchers', by the fact that in Bishops' Registers, charters, etc., rural churches are usually referred to by their geographical place-name, not by the dedication. (In towns containing several churches the use of the dedication had to be retained for purposes of identification.) In Willis's day 'parish feasts' were still being held, in spite of the repressive efforts of Reformers and Puritans, but they were limited to one a year, and might be held on the date of either the old Patronal Festival or the Dedication Festival. Willis seized with eagerness on the dates of the 'parish feasts' as giving unbroken evidence of the patron saint. This might be so if it was the date of the Patronal Festival which was being celebrated, but not if it was the Dedication Festival, which could fall anywhere in the year, and was indeed often moved (with episcopal permission) to a more convenient time in the agricultural or seasonal year. (Orme has found that in the Devon churches where both the mediaeval dedication and the date of the 18th-century parish feast are known, these coincide in only about 30 per cent of the cases. This indicates with what caution Willis's and Ecton's records of dedications should be approached.)

In the 19th century interest in dedications and patron saints increased, particularly under the influence of the Tractarian Movement. As a result of the feeling that every church should have a dedication, some retained or rediscovered their mediaeval ones, some accepted erroneous 18th-century conjectures, and when all else failed, some incumbents on their own authority invented dedications. In Herefordshire this appears to have been the case at Ford, for which see p.51. In another well-documented and more recent example, the church at Little Cowarne had lost its ancient dedication and was without one until 1992, when the Bishop of Hereford dedicated the church to St Guthlac, to commemorate the fact that it had been a possession of St Guthlac's Priory at Hereford.

In 1899 Frances Arnold-Forster published a 3-volume work entitled *Studies in Church Dedications, or England's Patron Saints*. This gave exhaustive statistical and iconographical information about dedications as they were at that time, but made no attempt to authenticate their historical pedigrees. This makes her book useless as a source for pre-Reformation dedications. Francis Bond in his *Dedications and Patron Saints of English Churches* published in 1914 recognised that many current dedications were recent substitutions and that many mediaeval ones had been lost. He urged the need for investigation of pre-Reformation wills and documents, but made little attempt to pursue such research himself. His lists therefore have no more historical validity than Arnold-Forster's. Until 1996 the one scholarly attempt to tackle the subject was a survey of the churches in the diocese of Carlisle by Graham and Collingwood published locally in 1925. But no future study of dedications can ignore Professor Nicholas Orme's *English Church Dedications, with a Survey of Cornwall and Devon*, published in 1996. The form and scope of this work have been outlined in the Preface.

Finally it should be noted that the present study has been limited (with very few exceptions) to parish churches in the administrative county of Herefordshire. It does not cover monastic institutions, except where the church survives in use, nor non-parochial chapels. In mediaeval times these latter were numerous, but in most cases they now survive only as a name on the map or in a documentary reference. Their dedications, where known, are often of considerable interest, but these chapels must await full treatment.

THE PATRON SAINTS

Feast Days are given in italics.

ALKMUND (1) *19th March*
Born *c*.774, Alkmund was the son of Alchred, King of Northumbria. The kingdom was seized by Eardwulf, who pursued Alkmund to Lilleshall in Shropshire, where he had taken refuge, and had him murdered there. (Another source—Higden's *Polychronicon*—says that he was killed in a battle near Cricklade in Wiltshire.) Alkmund was a Christian who met a violent death (*cp.* Clydog and Ethelbert) but can hardly be said to have 'died for his faith'. However he was claimed as a martyr and miracles were reported at his tomb in Lilleshall. His body was later translated to Derby and his shrine and holy well there became a place of pilgrimage. Several churches were dedicated to him in Derbyshire and Shropshire. The reason for his single dedication in Herefordshire—at Aymestrey—is unknown.

ALL SAINTS (9) *1st November*
A favourite dedication of Henry VIII which, in some cases, may have superseded dedications to obscure local saints.

ANDREW (14) *30th November*
Died *c*.60. Andrew, Apostle and Martyr, was a brother of Simon Peter and was the first disciple to be called by Christ (*John i, 40-41*). He does not play a very prominent part in the Gospel narratives, but later legends attribute many miracles to him and martyrdom by crucifixion at Patras in Greece. (His saltire cross does not appear until later.) In the 8th century some of his relics were said to have been taken by St Rule (Regulus) to Scotland, where St Andrew's in Fife became a religious centre and place of pilgrimage. Andrew was adopted as patron saint of Scotland, and his popularity among the apostles in English dedications was second only to St Peter.

The Virgin Mary, St Anne and the donor, Thomas Spofford; Ross-on-Wye

ANNA (1)   26th July
The first mention of Anna (Anne) as the mother of the Blessed Virgin Mary occurs in an apocryphal gospel of the 2nd century, her husband being named as Joachim. She is usually depicted in mediæval art seated and teaching her young daughter Mary to read. Unfortunately no such representation has survived at Thornbury, the sole church in Herefordshire dedicated to her. She is sometimes associated with springs and wells; there are 'healing wells' which bear her name at Aconbury and Malvern and at Buxton in Derbyshire.

BARNABAS (2)   11th June
An early disciple but not one of the Twelve, Barnabas accompanied Paul on his first missionary journey, but later quarrelled with him (*Acts xv, 39*) and went to Cyprus, which he evangelised. Later tradition says that he was martyred there. In England there are only seven pre-Reformation dedications to him, of which Brampton Bryan is one, but he became much more popular as a patron in the 19th century.

BARTHOLOMEW (8)   24th August
In the Gospels, Bartholomew is merely a name, unless—as many scholars suggest—he is identified with Nathanael (*John i, 45-51*) His legendary 'Acts'

recount missionary work and miracles in India, and martyrdom by being flayed alive—hence the flaying knife which is his emblem in mediæval art. For some reason he enjoyed great popularity in the Middle Ages—possibly because of the gift of one of his arms to Canterbury by the wife of King Cnut in the 11th century—and 165 churches were dedicated to him. (The flaying knife with Bartholomew's name is shown on a shield in the Stanbury Chapel in Hereford Cathedral.)

BEUNO (1)   *21st April*
According to a 14th-century 'Life', Beuno was born in Powys *c*.560 but brought up in Gwent. The King of Gwent, struck by his piety, gave him some land in Ewyas and there, at what is now Llanveynoe, he built a monastery. Beuno then returned to Powys and spent the rest of his life in North Wales, where many religious foundations are attributed to him, the most notable being at Clynnog Fawr in Caernarvonshire. He died and was buried there, and miracles were reported at his shrine. Butler regrettably describes this 'Life' as 'a fantastic narrative which merits no confidence.' Beuno's little church at Llanveynoe high above the Olchon valley was rededicated to St Peter at some date unknown, but Beuno has now been reinstated as a joint patron.

BRIDGET (1)   *1st February*
Bridget, Brigid or Bride (*c*.453-523) was a favourite Irish saint. She is said to have been baptised by St Patrick, and later founded many convents, of which that at Kildare became the most famous. There are few facts known about her life, but a wealth of legends. One of these, to illustrate her unworldliness, tells how she hung her cloak on a sunbeam, taking it for a clothes line. Her cult spread to Wales and England and about 20 churches were dedicated to her in each country, the best known English one being St Bride's in Fleet Street, London. Her sole Herefordshire dedication is at Bridstow.

CATHERINE (1)   *25th November*
Catherine is supposed to have lived in Alexandria in the 4th century, but all the accounts of her life are completely unhistorical. Legends recount that she was of royal birth and vowed to chastity, that she rejected the advances of the Emperor Maxentius, that she refuted the arguments of the 50 philosophers sent to persuade her of the error of her beliefs, and that she was tortured on the spiked wheel which is her emblem in ancient art and which gave her name to the popular firework. She was then beheaded, and her body was miraculously transported to a monastery on Mount Sinai. Under the influence of the

St Catherine, left from Old Radnor, right from Ludlow

Crusaders her cult spread all over Europe, and 62 churches were dedicated to her in England. Many of these are on hilltops, including the single Herefordshire example at Hoarwithy, because of her association with Mount Sinai.

Note: St Katherine's Hospital at Ledbury was founded in 1252 and is dedicated to St Catherine of Alexandria, not, as popularly supposed, to 'Saint' Katherine of Ledbury. This local and historical figure, Lady Katherine Audley (b.1272), attained fame as a recluse and became associated with a collection of legends, but was never canonised—and in any case the hospital was founded before her birth.

THE PATRON SAINTS

CEWYDD (1?) — *2nd July*

An obscure Radnorshire saint, where two churches—Aberedw and Disserth—are dedicated to him. He is said to have lived as a hermit in a cave at Aberedw Rocks, near Builth Wells. His sole claim to fame is that he was the Welsh equivalent of St Swithin. According to tradition, if it rains on Cewydd's feast-day (2nd July) it will rain for the next 40 days; hence he was known as *Hen Gewydd y Gwylaw* (Old Cewydd of the Rain). His name is held by local historians to be commemorated in Cusop (*Cheweshope* in Domesday). It is assumed that he founded the church there, and that it was originally dedicated to him, for the parish feast was held on the second Sunday in July. This date has no relevance to the present dedication to St Mary, which may be a result of the Norman purging of local saints. But this derivation from Cewydd has been questioned—see Appendix I.

CHRIST CHURCH (3)

The three Herefordshire dedications are all modern foundations—Llangrove, Llanwarne (new church) and Wellington Heath.

CLYDOG (1) — *3rd November*

Clydog was a Prince of Ewyas in the 5th or 6th Century, and was the son or grandson of Brychan, King of Brycheiniog (Brecknock), who sired many saints. A nobleman's daughter fell in love with Clydog, and he was murdered by a jealous rival while out hunting. His body was placed on an ox-cart, but the yoke broke while the cart was crossing the Monnow, and the oxen refused to go any further. The prince's body was laid on the west bank of the river, and immediately a spring burst forth on the spot (*cp.* Ethelbert). He was buried there, and a chapel built over his grave. This became a place of miracles and is the site of the present church of Clodock, which perpetuates his name.

CONSTANTINE (1) — *9th March*

The complicated history of Welsh Bicknor church is set out in Appendix I. The Constantine who presumably founded the church at *Lanncustenhinn* is described in the *Book of Llandaff* as a king and the father-in-law of King Peipiau (see Dyfrig). Whether he is to be identified with the 6th-century Constantine to whom churches were dedicated in Cornwall and Devon is uncertain—though not impossible, in view of the frequent saintly traffic between Wales and Cornwall. If they are to be identified, *Llancerniu*, otherwise *Cenubia Cornubium*,[1] that is, 'the Cornishmen's church', may also have been founded by Constantine. This was in the Dore valley, and may be the present site of Abbey Dore.[2]

SAINTS IN HEREFORDSHIRE

COSMAS & DAMIAN (1) *26th September*
(Date unknown: possibly 4th century.) Legend describes Cosmas and Damian as two young Arab doctors, possibly twin brothers, who lived in Cilicia and were martyred for refusing to sacrifice to idols. They treated animals as well as human patients, and took no fees for their services. With St Luke they are the patron saints of doctors. Only five churches in England are dedicated to them, one of which is Stretford near Leominster. This little church, now redundant, but well cared for, contains a 'shrine' which is said to have held relics of the saints. In 1538 offerings at this shrine were estimated to bring in £2 0s 6d annually—half the total income of the Rector of Stretford. There are also records of a healing well near the church, but the site of this is now lost. At some time unknown the ancient dedication also was lost, and the church rededicated to St Peter (*cp*. Llanveynoe), but Cosmas and Damian have recently been reinstated as patrons.

CUTHBERT (1) *20th March*
One of the great saints of the north of England, Cuthbert's life (634-687) is recorded by Bede. Brought up at Melrose Abbey, he was appointed Prior of Lindisfarne but soon withdrew to a hermitage on the Farne Islands, off the Northumberland coast. He was recalled to become Bishop of Lindisfarne and died there. His body was eventually transferred to Durham, where his tomb in the cathedral became a famous object of pilgrimage. Over 100 churches are dedicated to him in the north of England, but the sole dedication in Herefordshire is at Holme Lacy. There was a northern branch of the Lacy family, and there was an 8th-century bishop of Hereford called Cuthbert, but the reason for this dedication remains obscure.

CYNIDR (1) *8th December*
Cynidr now has no church dedicated to him in Herefordshire, but Kenderchurch, now dedicated to St Mary, preserves his name (Kenderchurch = Llangynidr), and he must have originally been its patron and probably founder. He, like Clydog, was the son or grandson of King Brychan, and founded several churches in Breconshire, including Glasbury, where he was buried. Cynidr is sometimes described as a bishop, and Kenderchurch was possibly the seat of a bishopric between the 6th and 10th centuries. He also established a hermitage on an island in the Wye near Winforton. Blount (1675) writes 'Temp: Bp. Hugh Foliot, Walter, a Canon of Wormesley Priory, betook himself to an Eremetical Life in a little island upon the River Wey (sic) ... (which Island is called by the Inhabitants "Hermit Island") wherein ... he built a Chappel dedi-

cated *deo beatae Mariae, beato Kenedro* - a Saxon saint as I suppose - and afterwards it usually bore the name of St Kendred's Chapel.' Blount lists several subsequent benefactors to this chapel. He continues 'The church [Winforton] I suppose is also dedicated to the before-mentioned St Kendred, for they keep their feast of dedication at an unusual time, viz: a little before Christmas. The place where St Kendred's Chapel stood is yet called the Chapel Close, where the foundation stones have been lately digged up, and where yet stands an Yew tree, and the place is only surrounded by the River Wey in the Tyme of a flood.'

DAVID (4)   *1st March*

It is strange that so few facts are known about the life of the most famous of the Welsh saints, 'Dewi Sant', though there is no lack of legends, which are collected in a 'Life' written in 1095. He is said to have founded ten monasteries, including Glastonbury and Menevia (St David's). He is also said to have succeeded Dubricius (*q.v.*) as Archbishop of Caerleon, and to have transferred the episcopal see of South Wales to St David's, where his monastery church became the cathedral. (The Welsh archbishopric was never recognised by Rome.) He died there *c*.588 and his shrine became a famous object of pilgrimage. The Herefordshire churches dedicated to David—Kilpeck, Much and Little Dewchurch and perhaps Dewsall (though this dedication is now to St Michael)—may in fact have been founded by an earlier and lesser-known priest called Dewi, whose memory was obliterated by the renown of his greater namesake. (A 7th-century charter in the *Book of Llandaff* refers to '*devi summus sacerdos*' *i.e*. David the Chief Priest.)[3]

DEINST (1)   *11th September*

Better known as Deiniol, he possibly founded the monastery at Bangor Iscoed on the Dee, and certainly the one at Bangor Fawr on the Menai Straits. He was consecrated bishop by Dubricius (*q.v.*), or according to another tradition by David, and is regarded as the first bishop of Bangor. He died *c*.584 and was buried on Bardsey Island, 'the Island of Saints'. Tradition relates that he founded the church at Llangarron in Herefordshire, the only church in England dedicated to him (there is another at Itton in Gwent, formerly known as Llandeiniol).

DENYS (2)   *9th October*

The history of St Denys, Dennis or Dionys, patron saint of France, is complicated by several incompatible traditions. Most probably he was born in Italy in the 3rd century and sent by the Pope with five companions to convert France. He established a Christian centre where Paris now stands, but suffered martyrdom by beheading. Over his tomb was built the great abbey of St Denis, the later burial-place of the French kings. He is claimed as the first bishop of Paris, and in mediæval art is represented as a bishop holding a crozier in one hand and his severed head in the other. His cult became popular in England, doubtless owing to Norman influence, and over 40 churches were dedicated to him. Only two are in Herefordshire, at Harewood (the church is disused) and Pencoyd.

DYFRIG/DUBRICIUS (8) *14th November*

Dyfrig (Latinised as Dubricius, Normanised as Devereux) was the greatest of the Herefordshire saints, who in the 6th century evangelised the kingdom of Archenfield (Ergyng)—the southern part of Herefordshire—the name of which is perpetuated in the Deanery of Ross and Archenfield. Although a historical figure, Dyfrig's life, which is recounted in the *Book of Llandaff*, has been enriched and obscured by legend, not least in the story of his birth at Madley. One day Peipiau, King of Ergyng, noticed that his daughter Ebrdil was pregnant. In anger he ordered her to be tied in a sack and thrown into the Wye. Each time she was thrown into the river she was miraculously swept back to the bank, so in frustration the king ordered her to be burnt alive on a pyre. This attempt also failed, for the girl would not catch alight—possibly because of her recent immersion. The king then appears to have given up his murderous intentions, for next day Ebrdil was found nursing a new-born son who, because of his ante-natal ordeal, she named Dyfrig—'water baby'. Peipiau, struck by remorse, took the infant in his arms. The child stretched up and touched his grandfather's face, thereby miraculously curing him of a distressing affliction from which he suffered—a perpetual foaming at the mouth.

Little is known of Dyfrig's early life, but he founded a number of churches, monasteries and schools, chief among them being the colleges at Hentland (Hen-llan = old church) and Moccas. There are records of many grants of land made to him for this purpose by local rulers, including King Peipiau, who owed Dyfrig a debt of gratitude for his miraculous cure. Dyfrig and his many disciples were active in spreading Christianity throughout Archenfield and Gwent. He is said to have been the first bishop of Llandaff, and also archbishop of Caerleon, in which office he was succeeded by St David, who moved the see to Menevia (St David's). These stories however raise acute historical difficulties.

Dyfrig spent his last years as a hermit on Bardsey Island (North Wales) and died there *c*.546. In 1120, to give colour to Llandaff's somewhat dubious claim that Dyfrig was its first bishop, his remains were translated to the cathedral there and enshrined with great pomp.

It may appear surprising that only five Herefordshire churches are dedicated to such a notable figure in the county's religious history—Hentland, Ballingham, Whitchurch, St Devereux and Hamnish (a 19th-century foundation). However, others of his churches have had their dedication changed, *e.g.* Llanwarne, originally dedicated to SS Dyfrig and Teilo, and Madley, which is said to have been originally dedicated to Dyfrig's mother Ebrdil, then to Dyfrig himself.

EDITH (1?)

Stoke Edith presents a problem, for details of which see Appendix I. There are confusingly several Anglo-Saxon Ediths who were given the title of Saint. The best known is Edith of Wilton (961-984). She was an illegitimate daughter of King Edgar by a nun of Wilton Abbey, near Salisbury. She was brought up at Wilton, and became renowned for her learning, charity and piety. The King wished to appoint her abbess of Barking and other abbeys, but Edith refused and remained at Wilton until her early death at the age of 23. Miracles took place at her tomb, and she became patroness of the great abbey of Wilton.

A brass of St Ethelbert from Hereford Cathedral

Queen Edith, wife of Edward the Confessor and sister of King Harold, was also given the title of Saint, and there was a third St Edith of Polesworth - but she does not concern us here.

ETHELBERT (1)   20th May

King of the East Angles, was one of the 'martyrs', like Alkmund and Clydog, who were not executed for their faith, but as young Christian princes were murdered for reasons of politics or passion, and attained sainthood by reason of the miracles recorded at their tombs. Ethelbert wished to marry Aelfthryth, daughter of Offa, King of Mercia. In 794 he visited Offa at his court at Sutton Walls, near Marden, and was there murdered at the instigation of Offa's queen, whether for reasons of jealousy or politics is not clear. His body was first buried at Marden, where a spring miraculously burst forth (it can still be seen at the west end of the church). The body was later transferred to Hereford, where the cathedral is dedicated to him jointly with the Blessed Virgin Mary. Many miracles of healing are said to have taken place at this tomb, which became an object of pilgrimage; there was also a holy well bearing his name to the east of the cathedral.

FAITH (2)   6th October

Faith (Foy) lived and died at Agen in south-west France in the 3rd century. Her story follows the usual pattern of virgin martyrs, except for the macabre method of her execution—she is said to have been roasted to death on a brass bedstead. The cult of Sainte Foy became remarkably popular and widespread in the Middle Ages, chiefly because her shrine at Conques (to which her relics were translated $c.870$) was on the pilgrim route to Santiago de Compostela. There are chapels dedicated to St Faith in Westminster Abbey and St Paul's Cathedral. It has been suggested that the two Herefordshire churches of which she is patron—Bacton and Dorstone, both in the Golden Valley—may in fact owe their dedications not to Sainte Foy of Agen but to a Celtic disciple of Dubricius called Tyfoi ($q.v.$) or Foi, whose name led to confusion with the better known saint, as occurred at Foy near Ross-on-Wye (see Appendix I).

FRANCIS (1)   4th October

Francis, the founder of the Franciscan Order of Friars, was born at Assisi in 1181, the son of a wealthy cloth-merchant. He joined his father's business, and became a leader of the young society of the town. He was however taken prisoner in a local war, and soon after suffered a serious illness. These experiences had a profound effect on him. To his father's extreme annoyance Francis decided to renounce all material comforts and lead an ascetic life. Gradually a group of like-minded disciples joined him, and Francis drew up a simple Rule for them, which was approved by the Pope in 1210. The Order rapidly increased in numbers,the brothers going out on preaching missions, and returning to a life of poverty and prayer at their communal house at Assisi.

    By 1220 the Order had grown to over 5,000 friars, with houses all over Italy and beyond. This necessitated a revision of the Rule, which included the establishment of Tertiaries—laymen who followed the Franciscan ideal, but lived with their families. Many stories are told of Francis, including the well-known one of his preaching to the birds, and many miracles were attributed to him, including the reception of the Stigmata (the marks of Christ's crucifixion) on his own body. He died in 1226 aged only 45, and was canonised two years later.

THE PATRON SAINTS

Franciscan (Grey) Friars came to England in 1224, and within a century they had established 50 houses in towns throughout the land, including one at Hereford, of which only the name 'Greyfriars' survives. Because of his comparatively late date, few mediaeval churches other than the Franciscan Friaries were dedicated to him, but the 20th century saw a widespread revival of his cult, with many modern dedications to St Francis, including one in the suburbs of Hereford.

GEORGE (4) *23rd April*
It is strange that our national patron saint should be one of whom so little is known. Tradition relates that George was a Roman soldier martyred in Palestine during the persecutions of the Roman Emperor Diocletian, in about 300 AD. The story of the princess and the dragon is, regrettably, unhistorical. According to this legend a dragon was terrorising the countryside with its poisonous breath, and had to be appeased by the annual offering of a human victim, chosen by lot. George happened to arrive in the neighbourhood on the day when the lot had fallen on the king's daughter. Protected by the sign of the Cross, George attacked the dragon, disabled it with a spear-thrust and led it back to the city bound with the princess's girdle. George told the rejoicing king and his people that if they would embrace Christianity he would rid them of the dragon for ever. When they agreed, he cut off its head, whereupon no less than 15,000 people accepted baptism.

George's popularity in England dates from the Crusades, when Richard I put his army under St George's protection, but George did not finally supplant Edward the Confessor as Patron Saint of England until the 14th century, when Edward III founded the Order of the Garter under George's patronage. Over 160 mediæval churches are dedicated to him throughout the country.

GILES (6) *1st September*
Giles, alias Egidius, who died *c*.700, is another very popular saint about whom little is reliably known. He is however the subject of various inconsistent legends. According to the best-known he lived as a hermit in a forest in the south of France, where he was attended by a hind which supplied him with milk. One day the hind was pursued by a royal hunting party, and took refuge in Giles's cave. One of the knights shot an arrow which accidentally struck and wounded Giles. The king came to the cave and was so impressed by Giles's sanctity and humility that he tried to persuade him to come to the royal court. Giles refused, but later founded a monastery in Provence which grew into the great abbey of St Gilles and became a famous place of pilgrimage. Giles is usually represented as an abbot holding a crozier with his hind at his feet. He became the patron saint

of cripples and lepers, and in England over 150 churches and many hospitals, including one in Hereford, were dedicated to him.

GOOD SHEPHERD (1)
This is always a modern dedication.

GUTHLAC (2) *11th April*
Guthlac (c.673-714) was of Mercian royal blood. After a distinguished career as a soldier he entered the monastery of Repton in Derbyshire but later withdrew to a hermitage in the fens near Crowland. There he lived a life of extreme austerity, being tempted by devils and consoled by angels, and gaining a great reputation for sanctity. After his death his shrine at Crowland Abbey became an object of pilgrimage and his cult spread all over England. The priory of St Guthlac within the castle at Hereford was in 1143 amalgamated with the priory of St Peter and moved to a new site outside the city walls where the County Hospital now stands, under the joint patronage of SS. Peter and Guthlac. (A chapel of St Guthlac in the castle survived the removal of the priory, and was described by Leland c.1535 as 'a faire Chappel'.) The original priory may have been founded in the reign of King Aethelbald (8th century) whose patron was St Guthlac; which might explain the dedication. The former chapel of the County Hospital was dedicated to St Guthlac, but with the move to a new building this has lapsed.

An unusual event took place in 1992 at Little Cowarne, where the mediæval parish church, of which the original dedication—if there ever was one—has been lost, was dedicated by the Bishop of Hereford to St Guthlac, to commemorate the fact that the church was in early times appropriated to St Guthlac's Priory at Hereford.

HOLY ROOD (1) *14th September*
The Great Rood, a figure of the crucified Christ flanked by the Blessed Virgin and St John, standing on the rood-beam in front of or above the chancel arch, was the dominating feature of the interior of every mediæval church, but not one survived the order of Edward VI in 1548 that all roods should be destroyed. As a dedication it is uncommon, the only example in Herefordshire being at Mordiford.

HOLY TRINITY (6) *Sunday following Whitsunday*
The Holy Trinity is represented emblematically in mediæval art in two ways: (i) pictorially, by a seated figure of God the Father holding His crucified Son

on His knees, with the Holy Ghost in the form of a dove hovering over His head, and
(ii) diagrammatically, showing the relationship between the Three Persons by the figure alongside.

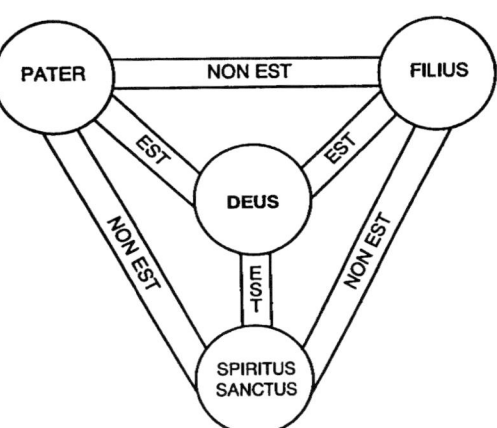

Thomas à Becket had a special devotion to the Holy Trinity, and instituted the festival of Trinity Sunday. Many dedications to the Holy Trinity date from his time. King Henry VIII also strongly favoured the dedication to the Holy Trinity, and caused it to be added to the dedications of many cathedrals. From his time to the end of the 17th century there was a reaction against saints in general, and non-biblical saints in particular, so dedications or re-dedications to the Holy Trinity are frequent during this period.

JAMES (12)

1. JAMES THE GREAT — 25th July

The son of Zebedee and brother of John, James was a leading apostle. His execution by Herod Agrippa in 44 is related in *Acts ii, 12*. In spite of this, there is a strong legend that he preached the Gospel in Spain, or at least that his body was miraculously carried there, and that he was buried at Santiago de Compostela. This became one of the most famous places of pilgrimage in Europe, and St James is usually but illogically represented as a pilgrim, with wallet, staff and a scallop-shell in his hat—a pilgrim, as it were, to his own shrine.

In 1126 King Henry I, the founder of Reading Abbey, presented to the abbey the reputed hand of St James. This relic attained great fame and many miracles were attributed to it. Leominster Priory was a dependency of Reading Abbey, and may have encouraged the cult of St James in Herefordshire.

2. JAMES THE LESS — 1st May

A problematical figure who has been identified with the apostle James, son of Alphaeus *(Matthew x, 3)*, the first head of the church in Jerusalem. He was beaten to death in about the year 60 with a fuller's club, which is his usual emblem. The authorship of the Epistle of James is sometimes attributed to one or other of these. James often shares a dedication with the apostle Philip, and their joint feast-day is 1st May. In Herefordshire there is one dedication to SS

Philip and James, but none specifically to St James the Less. The 12 dedications are either to James the Great or just 'St James'; some of these latter may refer to James the Less.

JOHN THE BAPTIST (24)   *24th June*

John Baptist is one of the few saints whose whole life-history is covered by the Gospels, in which full accounts of his birth, mission and death can be found. He is usually represented as unkempt, dressed in skins, with a lamb (often the *Agnus Dei* with its banner) in allusion to his greeting of Christ, 'Behold the Lamb of God'.

St John Baptist was extremely popular in the Middle Ages, surpassing all the apostles except Peter and Andrew, and in England alone almost 500 ancient churches are dedicated to him. He was the patron of the Knights Hospitallers, and hence is sometimes known as St John of Jerusalem, as at Dinmore and Bolstone which belonged to that Order.

SS James and John; Dore Abbey

THE PATRON SAINTS

JOHN THE EVANGELIST (4) *6th May and 27th December*
A strong and ancient tradition holds that the apostle John, son of Zebedee and brother of James, was the author of the Fourth Gospel and the 'beloved disciple', though from early times this identification has been questioned. It is generally held that the General Epistles of John are by the author of the Gospel, but the Revelation of St John the Divine ('Divine' = theologian) is a different matter. *The Oxford Dictionary of Saints* cautiously comments 'The Revelation or Apocalypse, though also ascribed to [John the Apostle] is so different in thought, style and content from the genuine Johannine writings that John's personal authorship of it in any normally accepted sense seems unlikely.' After the Resurrection, John is described in the Acts as playing a leading part, with Peter and James, in the church at Jerusalem. Tradition then takes over, and confusion begins. John is said to have settled at Ephesus, where he spent the rest of his long life. A story relates that the priest of Diana at Ephesus challenged John to drink a poisoned cup. John rendered the poison harmless with a blessing, and drank the draught unscathed. Hence he is often shown holding a chalice with a snake, representing the poison, rising from it. As one of the Four Evangelists however his emblem is an eagle.

The author of the Apocalypse however clearly states that he wrote it on the island of Patmos (*Rev.i.9*) — and this is not all. St John's chief feast-day is 27th December. A secondary festival of St John *ante Portam Latinam* on 6th May commemorates an ancient legend that, during the persecutions of Domitian, the aged apostle was immersed in a vat of boiling oil outside the Latin Gate at Rome: he emerged unscathed, and was banished to Patmos. This legend obviously assumes that the apostle was the author of the Apocalypse, but if so, when was he at Ephesus? Any attempt to reconcile the various traditions is probably vain.

JUNABIUS / INABWY / DINABO (1) *Unknown*
The church at Llandinabo is dedicated to St Junabius. So many problems are associated with this dedication that they have been relegated to Appendix III, where they are treated fully.

KEYNE / CEIN (1) *8th October*
Keyne was a daughter of that great sire of saints, King Brychan (see Clydog). Like many of her brothers and sisters — the legendary number of whom varies from 11 to 62 — she migrated to Cornwall, where she is commemorated by the church, holy well and village of St Keyne. In Herefordshire she was the founder or patroness of the church at what is now Kentchurch, though the dedi-

cation was at some time changed to St Mary. In early days the parish was known as Llancein or St Keyneschurch, and is so given in a Bishop's Register of 1302. This became Keynchurch, then Kenchurch. There is a story that an early 19th-century squire insisted on the insertion of the T because his letters were frequently misdirected to Kenchester—but this may well be apocryphal.

LAURENCE / LAWRENCE (5)   *10th August*

In 258 the Emperor Valerian instigated a persecution of the Christian church in Rome. The bishop Sixtus was executed and Laurence, a young deacon, was arrested and ordered to hand over the treasure of the church. Having asked for a few days grace to collect it, he then produced, not the expected gold and silver, but a crowd of poor and sick people, saying 'These are the treasures of the church'. In exasperation the Prefect of the city of Rome condemned him to death, and he was roasted alive on a grid-iron, which is his usual emblem. Laurence was very popular up to the Reformation, and the wealth of legend embellishing the few known facts of his life is indicated by the great east window of St Laurence's Church, Ludlow, which contains 27 scenes from his life and posthumous miracles.

St Laurence; Ludlow Church

LEONARD (3)   *6th November*

Another very popular but equally unhistorical saint (6th century?), Leonard was said to be the godson of King Clovis of France. Clovis offered him a bishopric, but Leonard refused, and retired to a hermitage in the forest of Noblac near Limoges. One day Clovis was hunting in the forest with his pregnant wife, who was suddenly overtaken with labour-pains. They took refuge in Leonard's hermitage where, thanks to his prayers and assistance, the child was safely delivered. In gratitude Clovis offered Leonard as much land as he could ride round on a donkey in one night. With this endowment Leonard founded the abbey of Noblac, of which he was abbot until his death. He used his influence with the king to secure the release of many well-known prisoners-of-war and captives. Because of his obstetrical services to the queen Leonard is the patron saint of pregnant women, but he is better known as the patron of prisoners, and is usually represented as an abbot holding a broken chain or fetters.

LUKE (2) — *18th October*

Considering how frequently the Four Evangelists appear in mediæval art, it is surprising how few ancient churches are dedicated to them, with the notable exception of St John. 19th- and 20th-century dedications are however far more common. In Herefordshire there are only two dedications to St Matthew (Frome's Hill and Marstow), none to St Mark and two to St Luke (Stoke Prior and Ullingswick). Three of these four are Victorian churches, and the fourth, Ullingswick, an ancient foundation but a modern dedication.

Most of our information about Luke comes from the New Testament. He was a doctor (*Col. iv 14* 'the beloved physician') and the author of the Third Gospel and the Acts of the Apostles, both written in Greek. He accompanied Paul on some of his missionary journeys. Tradition has it that he was also a painter, so he is the patron of both doctors and artists. When shown as one of the Evangelists his symbol is an ox, often winged.

MARGARET OF ANTIOCH (3) — *20th July*

In spite of her great popularity, it is doubtful whether Margaret ever existed, for there is no historical basis for the legends about her. According to these she was the daughter of a nobleman of Antioch in Pisidia (Asia Minor) and was brought up as a Christian by her nurse. The pagan Governor of Antioch tried to marry or seduce her, and when she refused him, he abducted, imprisoned and tortured her. A fearsome dragon appeared in her prison cell and swallowed her. Margaret prayed and made the sign of the Cross, whereupon the dragon 'burst asunder' and Margaret emerged unscathed. She was then subjected to further torture to persuade her to abjure her faith, and finally, when she still refused, was beheaded. Her noble fortitude and devotion to her beliefs converted a crowd of 5,000 onlookers to Christianity.

Margaret's last words were said to be a prayer that anyone who built and dedicated a church in her name should be granted remission of his sins. This may go some way to explaining her popularity as a patron. Over 260 churches were dedicated to her in England, though there are only three in Herefordshire—Wellington, Welsh Bicknor and St Margaret's. Rather surprisingly for a Virgin Martyr she is the patroness of childbirth—possibly in reference to the mode of her deliverance from the belly of the dragon. In art she is shown holding a cross-headed staff, which she thrusts into the mouth of the dragon at her feet.

MARTIN (2) *11th November*
Unlike the apocryphal St Margaret, St Martin of Tours has his life-story authenticated by a trustworthy contemporary biography. He was born *c*.316 in Hungary, and served in the Roman army. One cold winter day while stationed at Amiens he took pity on a beggar in rags who was soliciting alms. Since Martin had no money with him, he drew his sword, cut his military cloak in half and gave half to the beggar. That night he saw in a dream Christ wearing the half-cloak which he had given to the beggar. Soon afterwards Martin left the army and became a disciple of Hilary, the famous Bishop of Poitiers. He then became a monk, and founded a community following a rule of great austerity. He was appointed Bishop of Tours by popular acclamation, but continued to live as a monk, gaining a great reputation for sanctity. During his long episcopate he preached the Gospel vigorously and founded numerous monasteries. He was credited with many miraculous acts, and after his death in 397 his tomb became a place of pilgrimage.

In view of Martin's great popularity it is surprising that there is now only one dedication to him in the county—the parish church in Hereford city. There was also a chapel of St Martin in Hereford Castle, described by Hugh de Lacy in 1154 as 'the chapel which my ancestors founded', but during the reign of Henry II its endowments were transferred to St Guthlac's Priory, and it is not heard of again. The first mention of the parish church of St Martin at the south end of the Wye Bridge is *c*.1200.[4] This mediaeval church was destroyed during the siege of the city in 1645, and was replaced in 1845 by the present church on the Ross road.

The old church at Marstow (*Lann Martin* 1130, *Martinstow* 1277) was dedicated to him, but the new church is dedicated to St Matthew.

MARY THE BLESSED VIRGIN (50) *25th March*
That part of the Blessed Virgin's life which is covered by the Gospels is illuminated by a number of episodes from the Annunciation to the Crucifixion. It is also extended at either end by both legend and dogma. Legend provides Mary with parents—Joachim and Anna—while dogma asserts her Immaculate Conception by her mother; this was proclaimed as an Article of Faith by Pope Pius IX in 1854. Mary's latter years are unrecorded, but from an early date

there was a tradition that instead of dying she had been taken up ('assumed') into Heaven, where she was crowned Queen of Heaven by her Son. The Assumption is also an Article of Faith in the Roman Church, proclaimed as such by Pius XII in 1950, though the Eastern Church celebrates instead her Dormition ('falling asleep').

The Blessed Virgin, as would be expected, surpasses all other saints in number of dedications. In the 13th and 14th centuries her cult was at its height; in cathedrals and larger churches new chapels were built in her honour, usually at the eastern end of the building, while in smaller churches a side chapel often became the Lady Chapel. In Herefordshire there are 50 churches dedicated to St Mary, in several of which her dedication seems to have replaced one to a local saint, *e.g.* Kentchurch. In mediæval times a number of festivals were celebrated in honour of the Blessed Virgin, notably the Conception, the Nativity, the Annunciation, the Visitation (or Salutation), the Purification and the Assumption. Blount (1675) gives four churches dedicated to the Assumption of the Blessed Virgin Mary (Almeley, Brilley, Eardisland and Pembridge) and four to the Nativity of the Blessed Virgin Mary (Dilwyn, Madley, Ross-on-Wye and Welsh Newton) and there may have been others, for most of the entries before the letter L in his MS are missing. Of these only Madley has retained its ancient dedication. Most churches dedicated to the Blessed Virgin Mary celebrate their patronal festival on 25th March — the Feast of the Annunciation, or Lady Day.

The Blessed Virgin Mary; Eaton Bishop

MARY MAGDALENE (8)   *22nd July*

Mary of Magdala is mentioned by name only three times in the Gospels as the woman out of whom Jesus cast seven devils (*Luke viii, 2*); as one of the women at the foot of the Cross; and as the one who found the tomb empty, and to whom Christ later appeared in the garden. She has also traditionally been identified with both Mary of Bethany, sister of Lazarus and Martha, and also with the 'woman who was a sinner', who wet Christ's feet with her tears, wiped them with her hair and anointed them with precious ointment. She was then told that her sins were forgiven her (*Luke vii, 37-50*). It might be thought that these last two identifications were mutually incompatible, but this does not seems to have been seen as an objection. Francis Bond remarks '[she] is indebted almost wholly for her renown to the pathetic episode in the Gospel wrongly attributed to her.'[5]

This remarkable confusion is illustrated by the fluctuating status of Mary Magdalene in the Prayer Book Calendar. In early Church Calendars major festivals were printed in red (hence our phrase 'red-letter day') with a special collect, epistle and gospel: minor festivals were in black, with no special Office for the day. From early times Mary Magdalene was a 'Red Letter' saint, with a collect referring to her as the sister of Lazarus. In 1549 a new collect was substituted, identifying her as the penitent sinner. In 1552 her name was struck out of the Calendar altogether. In 1561 she was reinstated, but as a 'Black Letter' saint with no collect; and finally in the Alternative Services Book of 1980 she reappeared as the equivalent of a 'Red Letter' saint, with a collect and gospel referring to her only as a witness of the Resurrection.

Her identification with Mary of Bethany gave rise to an extraordinary legend that she, Lazarus and Martha were put to sea by their enemies in a boat without oars or rudder, which miraculously brought them to land near Marseilles. There Lazarus ultimately became a bishop, while Mary spent the rest of her life in solitary contemplation in a hermitage at St Maximin, near Aix-en-Provence. An abbey was built on the site of her grave, which became a place of pilgrimage until it was destroyed by the Saracens in the 8th century. Mary's relics disappeared and it was claimed that they had been transported to the

Mary Magdalene with her pot of precious ointment; Sellack

great abbey of Vézelay in Burgundy. This claim was denied by the abbey of St Maximin, where a casket said to contain Mary's relics is still shown.

Mary Magdalene's popularity in pre-Reformation times was immense. Colleges at Oxford and Cambridge were dedicated to her, as well as 187 churches throughout England, of which eight are in Herefordshire. On the other hand, post-Reformation dedications are very rare—perhaps because in Protestant churches chastity is more highly regarded than contrition. Mary is usually represented in mediæval art as a penitent with long, flowing hair, holding her ointment pot.

MATTHEW (2) *21st September*
Matthew, one of the twelve apostles, has been generally accepted as the author of the First Gospel, which tells us that he was a tax-collector or customs officer working under the Romans, who left everything to follow the call of Christ. He is called Levi by Mark and Luke. There is an unreliable tradition of his mission and martyrdom in Ethiopia. As an Evangelist his symbol is a man (*Rev. iv, 7*), often shown as an angel. Mediæval dedications to Matthew are rare, but he became very popular, as did Mark and Luke, in the 19th century. The two Herefordshire churches dedicated to him (Fromes Hill and Marstow) are both of this date, though the old church at Marstow was dedicated to Martin.

St Michael weighing souls;
Eaton Bishop

MICHAEL (32) *29th September*
Michael the Archangel was the special guardian of the Jewish people, and appears in the Revelation of St John (*ii, 7-12*) as the leader of the heavenly hosts against the powers of evil, symbolised by the dragon. Since he had no earthly existence he was exempt from the usual biographical embellishments of legend, though he is

credited with some miraculous appearances. As the guardian, and indeed judge, of souls his intercession was highly regarded, and he is often shown holding the Scales of Justice in which souls are weighed before the Last Judgement. As captain of the spiritual forces of the Church against the powers of darkness he is also shown as a winged and feathered figure in armour with drawn sword, trampling the dragon underfoot. He was extremely popular in the Middle Ages, and in Herefordshire he is second only to the Blessed Virgin in number of dedications. (Some of these are to St Michael and All Angels, others to St Michael alone.) It is often said that churches dedicated to St Michael should be on hilltops, presumably because of his heavenly activities, and there are indeed some spectacular examples such as St Michael's Mount and Glastonbury Tor, but it is patently untrue of most of his churches in Herefordshire.

NICHOLAS (3) *6th December*
Nicholas was Bishop of Myra in Asia Minor in the 4th century. His 'Life' consists of a series of spectacular miracles and acts of charity rather than a historical account. Of the better-known legends, one tells how, while on a pilgrimage to the Holy Land, he responded to the prayers of some sailors threatened with shipwreck by calming the winds and waves; because of this he is the patron saint of sailors. On another occasion he secretly gave three bags of gold as marriage portions for the three daughters of an impoverished nobleman, to save them from prostitution; these are said to be the origin of the three golden balls on the signs of pawnbrokers, whose patron he also is. Most famously he restored to life three small boys whom a cannibalistic inn-keeper had murdered, chopped up and hidden in a pickling-barrel; because of this he is the patron saint of children, and the original of Father Christmas (Dutch *Sante Klaas*, Santa Claus). In some cathedrals, including Hereford, a chorister is still chosen as 'Boy Bishop' on St Nicholas' Day (6th December) and holds office until after Christmas.

St Nicholas is represented as a bishop, with either a ship or the three boys in the pickling-tub. He was enormously popular in the Middle Ages, with over 400 churches dedicated to him in England.

OWEN (1) *24th August*
His name is variously given as Audoen or Ouen in France, and Owen or Ewen in England. Owen (*c*.600-684) was brought up at the Frankish court and became Chancellor to two kings. He later became a monk, and was consecrated bishop of Rouen, gaining a high reputation for sanctity during his long episcopate. There are only five dedications to him in England—three to Owen, two to

THE PATRON SAINTS

Ewen. His church in Hereford was destroyed in the siege of 1645 and never rebuilt, although its name still survives in the title of the parish and in St Owen's Street.

PAUL (1) *25th January*

Paul's life-story from the time of his conversion is told in detail in the Acts of the Apostles, with cross-references from the Epistles. The biblical story leaves him at Rome, apparently under house arrest. Tradition then takes over, and relates that he made a further missionary journey to Spain and then returned to Rome, where he was eventually executed by order of the Emperor Nero in 64, hence his emblem of a sword.

Considering Paul's leading position in the early church, it is astonishing that so few ancient churches in England are dedicated to him—St Paul's Cathedral being a notable exception. The situation changes completely in more recent times. In England fewer than 40 churches were dedicated to Paul alone in the whole mediæval period, but over 200 in the 19th century. In Herefordshire there is only one dedication—the Victorian church at Tupsley. The 'Conversion of St Paul' is celebrated as his chief festival on 25th January (see also 'Peter and Paul').

PETER (20) *29th June and 1st August*

Simon, son of Zebedee and brother of Andrew, was given by Christ the nickname 'the Rock' (*Cephas* in Hebrew, *Petros* in Greek) and became a leader among the disciples. He appears frequently in the Gospels and in the early part of the Acts, but disappears from the narrative after James becomes President of the Church. A strong and early tradition tells that he went to Rome and became bishop of the church there, suffering martyrdom with St Paul in Nero's persecution of AD 64. It is said that he was, at his own request, crucified head downwards as a sign of humility.

Peter was invoked as the Gatekeeper of Heaven (his usual emblem is a pair of keys) and revered as the founder of the Church of Rome. Over 1,000 churches were dedicated to him in England, and in Herefordshire his total of 19 is surpassed only by St Mary, St Michael and St John Baptist. The festival of his martyrdom is celebrated on 29th June, and there is a subsidiary feast day of St Peter *ad vincula* (in chains) on 1st August, commemorating his miraculous release from prison (*Acts xii*).

PETER AND PAUL (5) *29th June*

While only about 40 ancient churches in England are dedicated to Paul alone, 283 have him as joint patron with St Peter. There is a tradition that they suffered martyrdom on the same day, and when joint patrons they share the festival on 29th June.

A pleasing but utterly unhistorical legend relates that Peter and Paul, on parole from their imprisonment at Rome, set out on a preaching mission first to Spain and then to Britain. They landed on the coast of Gwent, and made their way north to the Black Mountains, so originating the name of the Gospel Pass (*Bwlch-yr-Efengyl*) overlooking the upper Wye valley. Here they parted, Paul turning westward and Peter south-east down the Golden Valley. At what is now Peterchurch he blessed a spring or well for baptising his converts. To mark its hallowing he placed in it a fish attached to a golden chain, the effigy of which can still be seen in the church there. Unfortunately the legend gives us no information about the saints' subsequent travels, or how they found their way back to Rome to meet martyrdom.

SS Peter and Andrew; Dore Abbey

THE PATRON SAINTS

PHILIP AND JAMES (1) *1st May*
Philip is included in the list of Apostles in all four Gospels, but apart from that all we know of him comes from minor references by St John, including his involvement in the Feeding of the Five Thousand (*John vi, 7*). This explains why St Philip is usually represented carrying a basket of loaves. According to tradition, after spending his latter years on missionary work in Asia Minor he suffered martyrdom by crucifixion. The James with whom he is frequently associated—though there seems no obvious reason for the association—is James the Less (*q.v.*) and their joint festival is 1st May. The only Herefordshire dedication is Tarrington.

SILAS (1) *13th July*
Silas is mentioned several times in the Acts and Epistles as a companion of St Paul on some of his missionary journeys. Otherwise nothing is known of him, and no traditions have grown up round his name. Not surprisingly he has no mediæval dedications and one wonders why several Victorian church-builders chose him as their patron. His dedication at Bollingham presumably dates from the 19th-century rebuilding of the chapel.

SWITHIN (1) *15th July*
Swithin or Swithun was appointed Chancellor of England by King Egbert, and Bishop of Winchester by King Ethelwulf (father of King Alfred). He had great influence over both kings, and was noted for his charitable acts and for the number of churches that he founded. When he died in 862 he was buried at his own request outside the door of the Old Minster at Winchester. A hundred years later the bishop of the time wished to translate St Swithin's bones to a sumptuous tomb in the new cathedral, but this project was delayed by heavy rain which lasted for 40 days—presumably a sign of the saint's disapproval. This has given rise to the popular superstition that if it rains on St Swithin's Day (15th July) it will continue to rain for 40 days. Swithin's cult was popular and widespread, but the only dedication to him in Herefordshire is at Ganarew.

TEILO (2) *9th February*
An important 6th-century figure, whose work centred on the famous monastery which he founded at Llandeilo Fawr (Dyfed). He is said to have been a disciple of Dyfrig whom, after spending seven years in Brittany, he succeeded as Bishop of Llandaff. He died at Llandeilo Fawr, and his body was claimed by Penally (his birthplace), Llandaff and Llandeilo. It is said that the dispute was miraculously settled by his body being multiplied by three, so that each place

could have one. At any rate, relics of Teilo were venerated in each place, and his tomb and shrine in Llandaff Cathedral can still be seen; he shares the dedication of the cathedral with Dyfrig, Euddogwy, Peter and Paul. In Herefordshire the original dedications of the churches at Hentland and Llanwarne were jointly to Dyfrig and Teilo.

THOMAS OF CANTERBURY (2) — *29th December*

Thomas à Becket was born in London in 1118 of a wealthy Norman family. He studied Law in France and Italy and, becoming a protégé of Theobald, Archbishop of Canterbury, was appointed Archdeacon of Canterbury at the early age of 36. In the following year the young King Henry II appointed him Chancellor of England. He became a trusted friend and counsellor of the king, who appointed him Archbishop of Canterbury in 1162. Thomas had not sought this office, and accepted it unwillingly. He soon showed his independence by resigning the Chancellorship and adopting an austere way of life. He vigorously upheld the rights of the Church against the Crown, and a bitter struggle developed between the two former friends. Thomas felt obliged to withdraw to France for six years for his own safety. A truce was arranged in 1170 and Thomas returned to Canterbury, but the quarrel soon broke out again even more violently. In a rage King Henry asked his courtiers who would 'rid him of this turbulent priest'. Four knights took him at his word, and killed Thomas in his own cathedral.

The news of the archbishop's murder shocked Christendom. Miracles were reported at his tomb, and he

SS Thomas Becket and Cantilupe; Credenhill

was canonised in 1173. The king did public penance for his death, and the fame of the martyred saint spread all over western Europe. His tomb at Canterbury became a noted place of pilgrimage, and over 80 churches in England were dedicated to him.

Henry VIII regarded Thomas as a traitor rather than a martyr: he ordered that he should be referred to as 'Bishop Becket' rather than 'St Thomas of Canterbury', destroyed his shrine in Canterbury Cathedral, expunged his name from the Calendar, forbade any celebration of his festival, and ordered that all images and pictures of him in churches should be defaced. Of the churches dedicated to St Thomas of Canterbury some, in defiance of the king's orders, retained him as their patron, some converted their dedication to St Thomas the Apostle—or, non-committally, 'St Thomas'—while others chose one of the dedications particularly approved of by the king, such as All Saints or the Holy Trinity. The only surviving dedications in Herefordshire—though there may have been others—are at Much Birch (combined with St Mary) and at Huntington near Kington.

TWELVE SAINTS, THE (1)

The Twelve Saints (their names are given by Wrmonoc as: Iahoevius, Tigernomalus, Toseocus or Siteredus, Woednovius or Towoedocus, Gellocus, Bretowennus, Boius, Winniavus, Lowenanus, Toetheus or Tochicus, Chielus and Hercanus or Herculanus) appear to be twelve priests, disciples of St Paulinus (also known as Paul Aurelian), a follower of St Illtud. He founded a monastery at Llandeusant near Llandovery, and later went to Brittany, accompanied by the Twelve. There he became bishop of St Pol de Léon, giving his name to the see; his 'Life' was written by Wrmonoc, a Breton monk, in the 10th century. The *Book of Llandaff*[6] mentions a Well of the Twelve Saints—*Finnaun doudecseint*—near Llangorse in Breconshire, where the church is dedicated to St Paulinus. The church at Welsh Bicknor was originally dedicated to the Twelve (see Appendix I), but there is no other known dedication to them. Their presence in Archenfield is unexplained, since Paulinus is not known to have worked in that area.

TYSILIO (2?) *8th November*

Tysilio, a 7th-century Welsh saint, was a brother of Cynon, King of Powys, and cousin and successor of St Asaph as Abbot of Llanelwy (now St Asaph's). There are dedications to him all over Wales, but the only one in England is at Sellack. The Ty- is a detachable 'familiar' prefix, and his name also appears as Suliau and Siloc. The *Book of Llandaff*[7] records the consecration of the church at *Lannsuluc*, hence Sellack. Like Beuno and Deiniol, Tysilio is chiefly associated with north Wales, and particularly with Meifod in Powys. Since there is no record of his having visited Herefordshire, the reason for the Sellack dedication is obscure. Llancillo (*Lannsulbiu*) may also be a foundation of his, though the church there is now dedicated to St Peter.

TYVOI (3?) *Unknown*

The name is also found as Tyfai, Fwy, Foi and Moi. The first syllable, 'Ty', is detachable (see Tysilio), while initial F and M mutate in Welsh, *e.g.* Mair (Mary) but Llanfair (St Mary's church). Tyvoi was a disciple of Dyfrig (*q.v.*) and according to the *Book of Llandaff*[8] the church at *Lanntiuoi* (now Foy) was consecrated by Bishop Herwald 'at the time of Edward the Confessor'. By the 12th century, owing to a confusion between the Celtic saint's name and Sainte Foi, the dedication is described as St Faith (*q.v.*). At some later date it was changed again to its present style of St Mary. Mr B. Coplestone-Crow has suggested that the two dedications to St Faith in the Golden Valley—Bacton and Dorstone—may in fact be foundations by Tyvoi and subject to the same confusion as Foy.

WEONARD (1) *Unknown*

Nothing is known for certain about St Weonard, whose name also appears as 'Gwainerth' (AD 450) and 'Waynard' (1291). The Oxford Dictionary of Saints states that he was 'a Celtic monastic saint, possibly connected with Dyfrig (Dubricius)', but gives no evidence for this. The local tradition is that he was a hermit and a wood-cutter. Blount (1675) writes of St Weonard's Church 'I find in the North Window of the Chancel the Picture of an Ancient Man with a long beard, holding a book in one hand and an axe in the other and under written in old characters - S. Wenardus Heremyta. I suppose he was a British Saint and that the church was dedicated to him.' The figure in the present (1875) window obviously derives from this description. The church at St Weonard's is his only dedication in England, although Llanwenarth in Gwent probably preserves his name also.

References

In these references, the following notation is used:

LL: Evans, J.G. and J.Rhys (eds.) *The Text of the Book of Llan Dav* (1893) (References are given to the pages of this edition.)
TWNFC: Transactions of the Woolhope Naturalists' Field Club

The sources referred to, if not quoted in full, can be found in the Bibliography. For a discussion on the reliability of some of the directories, please also refer to the Bibliography.

The Dedication of Churches
1. *LL* 195
2. Bond, Francis p.2
3. Arnold-Foster, I, p.499

The Patron Saints
1. *LL* 192
2. Coplestone Crowe, B. p.20
3. *LL* 162a
4. S.H. Martin in *TWNFC* 1934 p.219-, and F.G. Heys in *TWNFC* 1960 p.343-
5. Bond, Francis p.49
6. *LL* 146
7. *LL* 275
8. *LL* 275

LIST A
ALPHABETICAL LIST OF DEDICATIONS BY PATRON SAINTS

This list includes a number of churches which are disused, secularised, redundant or in ruins; also those which have been demolished, or whose dedication has been changed. The status of each church can be found by reference to the 'List of Dedications by Parishes'.

In this list, italics denote a joint dedication; brackets denote that the dedication has been changed or the church demolished.

Alkmund (1)	*Aymestrey (with John Baptist)*
All Saints (9)	Bishopswood, Brockhampton-by-Ross, Clehonger, Coddington, Eyton, Hereford, Kinsham, Monkland, Yatton
Andrew (14)	Adforton, Allensmore, Bredenbury, Bredwardine, Bridge Sollars, Dinedor, Evesbatch, Hampton Bishop, *How Caple (with Mary)*, Moreton-on-Lugg, Leysters, Leinthall Earles, Pixley, Wolferlow
Anna (1)	Thornbury
Barnabas (2)	Brampton Bryan, Hereford
Bartholomew (9)	Ashperton, Docklow, Holmer, Much Marcle, Munsley, Richard's Castle, Thruxton, Vowchurch, Westhide
Beuno (1)	*Llanveynoe (with Peter)*
Bridget (1)	Bridstow
Catherine (1)	Hoarwithy
Christ Church (3)	Llangrove, Llanwarne (new church), Wellington Heath
Clydog (1)	Clodock

HEREFORDSHIRE SAINTS

Constantine (1)	(Welsh Bicknor - now Margaret)
Cosmas & Damian (1)	Stretford
Cuthbert (1)	Holme Lacy
Cynidr (1)	(Kenderchurch - now Mary)
David (4)	*Kilpeck (with Mary)*, Little Dewchurch, Much Dewchurch, (Dewsall ? - now Michael)
Deinst (1)	Llangarron
Denys (2)	(Harewood), Pencoyd
Dubricius (7)	Ballingham, Hamnish, Hentland, (Llanwarne old church - now John Baptist), (Madley - now Nativity of Blessed Virgin Mary), St Devereux, Whitchurch
Edith (1)	(Stoke Edith ? - now Mary)
Ethelbert (1)	*Hereford Cathedral (with Mary)*
Faith (3)	Bacton, Dorstone, (Foy - now Mary)
Francis (1)	Hereford
George (4)	Brinsop, Burrington, Orleton, Woolhope
Giles (6)	Acton Beauchamp, Aston, Downton, Edvin Loach (old church), Goodrich, Mansel Gamage
Good Shepherd (1)	Upper Colwall
Guthlac (2)	Little Cowarne, (Priory at Hereford)
Holy Rood (1)	Mordiford
Holy Trinity (6)	*Abbey Dore (with Mary)*, Bosbury, Brockhampton-by-Ross (old church), Hardwicke, Hereford, Preston Wynne
James (12)	Bartestree, Canon Frome, Colwall*, Cradley, Hereford, Kimbolton*, Kinnersley, Ocle Pychard*, Stanford Bishop, Tedstone Delamere*, Tedstone Wafre (new church), Wigmore
	* = James the Great
John Baptist (24)	Aconbury, Aston Ingham, *Aymestrey (with Alkmund)*, Bolstone*, Byford, Dinmore*, Eastnor, Ford*, Grendon Bishop, Hereford, King's Caple, Lea, Letton, Llanrothal, Llanwarne (old church), Mathon, Newton, Orcop, Storridge, Upton Bishop, Weston Beggard, Whitbourne, Yarkhill, Yazor (old church)
	* = John of Jerusalem

LIST A

John the Evangelist (4)	Howle Hill, Ivington, Pencombe, Shobdon
Junabius (1)	Llandinabo
Keyne (1)	(Kentchurch - now Mary)
Lawrence (5)	Bishopstone, Canon Pyon, Preston-on-Wye, Stretton Grandison, Weston-under-Penyard
Leonard (3)	Blakemere, Hatfield, Yarpole
Luke (2)	Stoke Prior, Ullingswick
Margaret (3)	St Margaret's, Wellington, Welsh Bicknor
Martin (2)	Hereford, (Marstow - old church)
Mary the Blessed Virgin (50)	*Abbey Dore (with Holy Trinity)*, Almeley, Avenbury, Bishop's Frome, Brilley, Burghill, Byton, Callow, Clifford, Collington, Craswall, Credenhill, Cusop, Dilwyn, Donnington, Eardisland, Edvin Loach, Elton, Fownhope, Foy, Hope-under-Dinmore, *Hereford Cathedral (with Ethelbert)*, *How Caple (with Andrew)*, Humber, Kenderchurch, Kentchurch, King's Pyon, *Kilpeck (with David)*, Kington, Linton, Little Birch, Madley*, Marden, Middleton-on-the-Hill, Monnington-on-Wye, Moorcourt, *Much Birch (with Thomas à Becket)*, Much Cowarne, Pembridge, Ross-on-Wye, Sarnesfield, Staunton-on-Wye, Stoke Edith, (Tedstone Wafre - old church), Tretire, Tyberton, Walterstone, Welsh Newton, Wormsley, Yazor (new church)

           * = Nativity of Blessed Virgin Mary

Mary Magdalene (8)	Brobury, Eardisley, Huntington (Hereford), Leinthall Starkes, Leintwardine, Stretton Sugwas, Turnastone, Willersley
Matthew (2)	Frome's Hill, Marstow
Michael (32)	Bockleton, Bodenham, Brampton Abbotts, Breinton, Brimfield, Castle Frome, Croft, Dewsall, Dulas, Eaton Bishop, Edwyn Ralph, Ewyas Harold, Felton, Garway, Hope Mansell, Kenchester, Kingsland, Kingstone, Knill, Ledbury, Lingen, Little Marcle, Lyonshall, Mansel Lacy, Michaelchurch,

HEREFORDSHIRE SAINTS

	Michaelchurch Escley, Moccas, Sollarshope, Sutton St Michael, Upper Sapey, Walford, Winforton
Nicholas (3)	Hereford, Norton Canon, Sutton St Nicholas
Owen (1)	(Hereford)
Paul (1)	Tupsley
Peter (20)	Birley, Bromyard, Bullinghope, Dormington, Hereford,(Ledbury - now Michael), Llancillo, *Llanveynoe (with Beuno)*, Longtown, Lucton, Lugwardine, Peterchurch, Peterstow, Pipe-cum-Lyde, Pudleston, Rowlstone, Staunton-on-Arrow, Titley, Withington, Wormbridge
Peter & Paul (5)	Eye, Leominster, Stoke Lacy, Weobley, Whitney-on-Wye
Philip & James (1)	Tarrington
Silas (1)	Bollingham
Swithin (1)	Ganarew
Teilo (2)	(Hentland), (Llanwarne)
Thomas of Canterbury (2)	Huntington (Kington), *Much Birch (with Mary)*
Twelve Saints, The (1)	(Welsh Bicknor - now Margaret)
Tysilio (2?)	Sellack, (Llancillo ? - now Peter)
Tyvoi (1)	(Foy - now Mary)
Weonard (1)	St Weonard's
No dedication or dedication unknown (7)	Amberley, Aylton, Brockhampton-by-Bromyard, Moreton Jeffries, Putley, Wacton, Yatton (old chapel)

LIST B
LIST OF PRESENT DEDICATIONS BY PARISHES

C.C.T. = in care of Churches Conservation Trust (formerly Redundant Churches Fund)
Dis. = disused
Ru. = ruined
Sec. = secularised
Dem. = demolished
* indicates an entry in Appendix I
+ indicates an entry in Appendix II

Parish	**Dedication**
Abbey Dore *	Holy Trinity and Mary
Aconbury *	John Baptist (Sec.)
Acton Beauchamp	Giles
Adforton	Andrew
Allensmore	Andrew
Almeley	Mary
Amberley	no dedication
Ashperton	Bartholomew
Aston	Giles
Aston Ingham	John Baptist
Avenbury	Mary (Ru.)
Aylton	unknown
Aymestrey *	John Baptist and Alkmund
Bacton	Faith
Ballingham	Dubricius

HEREFORDSHIRE SAINTS

Bartestree	James
Birley	Peter
Bishop's Frome	Mary the Virgin
Bishopstone	Lawrence
Bishopswood	All Saints
Blakemere	Leonard
Bodenham * +	Michael and All Angels
Bollingham	Silas
Bolstone	John of Jerusalem (Dis.)
Bosbury	Holy Trinity
Brampton Abbotts	Michael
Brampton Bryan +	Barnabas
Bredenbury	Andrew
Bredwardine	Andrew
Breinton	Michael
Bridge Sollars	Andrew
Bridstow	Bridget
Brilley	Mary
Brimfield	Michael
Brinsop	George
Brobury	Mary Magdalene (Sec.)
Brockhampton-by-Bromyard	no dedication
Brockhampton-by-Ross	Old church - Holy Trinity (Ru.). New church - All Saints
Bromyard *	Peter
Bullinghope	Peter
Burghill	Mary
Burrington	George
Byford	John Baptist
Byton	Mary
Callow	Mary (Dis.)
Canon Frome	James
Canon Pyon	Lawrence
Castle Frome	Michael
Clehonger *	All Saints
Clifford +	Mary
Clodock	Clydog
Coddington *	All Saints
Collington *	Mary : All Saints (Dem)

LIST B

Colwall	James the Great
Cradley	James
Craswall +	Mary
Credenhill	Mary
Croft *	Michael and All Angels
Cusop *	Mary
Dewsall *	Michael
Dilwyn	Mary
Dinedor	Andrew
Dinmore	John of Jerusalem (non-parochial)
Docklow	Bartholomew
Donnington	Mary
Dormington	Peter
Dorstone *	Faith
Downton	Giles - both old (Ru.) and new churches
Dulas	Michael
Eardisland	Mary
Eardisley	Mary Magdalene
Eastnor	John Baptist
Eaton Bishop	Michael and All Angels
Edvin Loach *	New church - Mary; Old church (Ru.) - Giles
Edwyn Ralph	Michael
Elton	Mary the Virgin
Evesbatch	Andrew
Ewyas Harold	Michael and All Angels
Eye	Peter and Paul
Eyton	All Saints
Fawley	John (Dis.)
Felton	Michael the Archangel
Ford *	John of Jerusalem
Fownhope +	Mary
Foy *	Mary
Fromes Hill	Matthew
Ganarew *	Swithin
Garway	Michael
Goodrich	Giles
Grafton	see Bullinghope
Grendon Bishop	John Baptist

HEREFORDSHIRE SAINTS

Hamnish	Dubricius
Hampton Bishop	Andrew
Hardwicke	Holy Trinity
Harewood	Denis (Ru. - non-parochial)
Hatfield	Leonard
Hentland *	Dubricius
Hereford	Cathedral - Mary and Ethelbert Holy Trinity, All Saints, Barnabas, Francis, Guthlac (Priory - Dem.), James, John Baptist (Cathedral precinct), Martin, Nicholas, Owen (Dem.), Peter
Hoarwithy	Catherine
Holme Lacy *	Cuthbert (C.C.T.)
Holmer	Bartholomew
Hope Mansell *	Michael
Hope-under-Dinmore	Mary the Virgin
How Caple *	Andrew and Mary
Howle Hill	John
Humber	Mary the Virgin
Huntington (Hereford)	Mary Magdalene
Huntington (Kington) +	Thomas of Canterbury
Ivington	John
Kenchester	Michael
Kenderchurch *	Mary
Kentchurch *	Mary
Kilpeck * +	Mary and David
Kimbolton	James the Great
King's Caple	John Baptist
Kingsland +	Michael
King's Pyon *	Mary the Virgin
Kingstone	Michael and All Angels
Kington	Mary
Kinnersley +	James
Kinsham	All Saints
Knill	Michael and All Angels
Lea +	John Baptist
Ledbury *	Michael and All Angels
Leinthall Earles	Andrew

LIST B

Leinthall Starkes *	Mary Magdalene
Leintwardine *	Mary Magdalene
Leominster * +	Peter and Paul (Priory)
Letton *	John Baptist
Leysters	Andrew
Lingen	Michael and All Angels
Linton	Mary
Little Birch	Mary
Little Cowarne	Guthlac (since 1992 - see 'Guthlac')
Little Dewchurch	David
Little Hereford	Mary Magdalene
Little Marcle	Michael and All Angels
Llancillo *	Peter (D.C.; originally Tysilio?)
Llandinabo	Junabius (see App.III)
Llangarron	Deinst
Llangrove	Christ Church
Llanrothal *	John Baptist (C.C.T.)
Llanveynoe *	Beuno and Peter
Llanwarne *	Old church - John Baptist (Ru.)
	New church - Christ Church
Longtown	Peter (Sec.)
Lucton *	Peter (Sec.)
Lugwardine *	Peter
Lyonshall +	Michael and All Angels
Madley * +	Nativity of the Blessed Virgin Mary
Mansel Gamage	Giles (Sec.)
Mansel Lacy	Michael
Marden *	Mary
Marstow	Old church (Dem.) - Martin
	New church - Matthew
Mathon *	John Baptist
Michaelchurch	Michael (C.C.T.)
Michaelchurch Escley	Michael
Middleton-on-the Hill	Mary the Virgin
Moccas +	Michael and All Angels
Monkland *	All Saints
Monnington-on-Wye	Mary
Moorcourt	Mary
Mordiford *	Holy Rood

HEREFORDSHIRE SAINTS

Moreton Jeffries	unknown (C.C.T.)
Moreton-on-Lugg	Andrew
Much Birch	Mary and Thomas of Canterbury
Much Cowarne +	Mary
Much Dewchurch	David
Much Marcle	Bartholomew
Munsley	Bartholomew
Newton	John Baptist
Norton Canon	Nicholas
Ocle Pychard *	James the Great
Orcop	John Baptist
Orleton *	George
Pembridge	Mary the Virgin
Pencoyd	Denys
Peterchurch	Peter
Peterstow	Peter
Pipe-cum-Lyde	Peter
Pixley	Andrew
Preston-on-Wye * +	Lawrence
Preston Wynne	Holy Trinity
Pudleston	Peter
Putley	unknown
Richards Castle	Bartholomew (C.C.T.)
Ross-on-Wye	Mary
Rowlstone	Peter
St Devereux *	Dubricius
St Margaret's	Margaret
St Weonard's	Weonard
Sarnesfield	Mary
Sellack	Tysilio
Shobdon *	John the Evangelist
Sollarshope	Michael
Stanford Bishop	James
Staunton-on-Arrow *	Peter
Staunton-on-Wye * +	Mary
Stoke Edith *	Mary
Stoke Lacy *	Peter and Paul
Stoke Prior *	Luke
Storridge	John the Evangelist

LIST B

Stretford *	Cosmas and Damian (C.C.T.)
Stretton Grandison *	Lawrence
Stretton Sugwas	Mary Magdalene
Sutton St Michael	Michael
Sutton St Nicholas	Nicholas
Tarrington *	Philip and James
Tedstone Delamere	James the Great
Tedstone Wafre	New church - James (Sec.)
	Old church - Mary (Ru.)
Thornbury	Anna
Thruxton +	Bartholomew
Titley	Peter
Tretire	Mary
Turnastone	Mary Magdalene
Tyberton	Mary
Ullingswick *	Luke
Upper Colwall	Good Shepherd
Upper Sapey	Michael
Upton Bishop	John Baptist
Vowchurch	Bartholomew
Wacton	unknown (Ru.)
Walford	Michael and All Angels
Walterstone	Mary
Wellington *	Margaret of Antioch
Wellington Heath	Christ Church
Welsh Bicknor *	Margaret
Welsh Newton	Mary
Weobley	Peter and Paul
Westhide	Bartholomew
Weston Beggard *	John Baptist
Weston-under-Penyard	Lawrence
Whitbourne	John Baptist
Whitchurch *	Dubricius
Whitney-on-Wye *	Peter and Paul
Wigmore +	James
Willersley	Mary Magdalene (Dis.)
Winforton * +	Michael and All Angels
Withington	Peter
Wolferlow	Andrew

HEREFORDSHIRE SAINTS

Woolhope *	George
Wormbridge	Peter
Wormsley	Mary (C.C.T.)
Yarkhill	John Baptist
Yarpole	Leonard
Yatton	All Saints (Chapel (C.C.T.) dedication unknown)
Yazor	Old church (C.C.T.) - John Baptist. New church - Mary

APPENDIX I

CHANGES AND VARIANTS OF DEDICATION

Present dedication is given in brackets immediately after the parish's name. For a discussion on the directories and the accuracy or otherwise of the information they give, please refer to the Bibliography.

ABBEY DORE (Holy Trinity and Mary) The abbey, like all Cistercian foundations, was dedicated to the Blessed Virgin Mary. The Holy Trinity was added when the building was reconsecrated after the Scudamore restoration in 1634. Lewis gives the joint dedication, but all the later directories and clergy lists give Mary alone, up to the *HDD* for 1987, from which time onwards the joint dedication is given.

ACONBURY (John Baptist) The parish church at Aconbury (now redundant and used as the diocesan furniture repository) was the church of a small convent founded in *c*.1232 by Margaret de Lacy. She intended it to be a house of Augustinian Canonesses, but unwisely entrusted the arrangements for establishing the convent to the Preceptor of the Knights Hospitallers at Dinmore. He, not surprisingly, installed a group of nuns of his own order. When Margaret discovered this she appealed to the Pope, but the Hospitallers counter-appealed. After a long and acrimonious dispute the matter was finally settled in 1237, with the Pope establishing the Augustinian Canonesses at Aconbury.

In the *Calendar of Charter Rolls 1226-1257* an entry for Aconbury refers to 'the convent at Aconbury founded in honour of John the Baptist'. This is not surprising as all the churches of the Hospitallers were dedicated to their Patron, St John of Jerusalem (*i.e.* John Baptist). Rees however shows the church as dedicated to St Catherine. To confuse things further, Duncumb writes 'For the Priory Church various dedications are given - St Catherine, Holy Cross, St Mary and St John.' Ecton and Bacon give John Baptist. Possibly Margaret de Lacy, after the eviction of the Hospitallers, had the church rededicated to St Catherine, but the old dedication survived in popular usage. Duncumb's reference to Holy Cross and St Mary may apply to altars or chantries in the church. Slater gives St Augustine, but this obviously refers to the patron of the canonesses. *PO* 1863 and *Kelly* 1870 give 'not known'.

AYMESTREY (John Baptist and Alkmund) Blount (1675) gives Alkmund alone. It is possible that the original dedication was to Alkmund and that John Baptist was added later. The 'B stream' give John Baptist alone.

BODENHAM (Michael and All Angels) According to the *Cartulary of Brecon Priory* and *Foliot* the church was dedicated to St Mary in the 12th-13th centuries (BCC pers. and *Foliot* 290). Ecton and Bacon give St Michael, and so do all 19th-century directories and clergy lists.

BROMYARD (Peter) In June 1384 Bishop Gilbert held an inquisition into the status (collegiate or portionary) of the churches of Bromyard and Ledbury, and in the record of it we find '*ecclesie beatorum Petri et Pauli de Ledbury et Bromyard.*' (*Bishop Gilbert's Register* for 1384). Blount also gives Peter and Paul for Bromyard, but all later references give Peter alone.

CLEHONGER (All Saints). The 'B stream' give Mary, but all reputable sources give All Saints.

CODDINGTON (All Saints). In 1231, after some rebuilding, Bishop Hugh Foliot dedicated the high altar to St Peter (and two others to the Blessed Virgin Mary and St Milburga) (*Bishop Bothe's Register* for 1527, p.199). This suggests that Peter was the original dedication of the church. Lewis and the 'A stream' give All Saints, but the 'B stream', surprisingly, Peter.

COLLINGTON (Mary) In 1352 the two parishes of Greater and Lesser Collington were so depopulated by plague that the inhabitants petitioned the Bishop of Hereford to unite the parishes. This was done, and as Little Collington church was more conveniently placed, this became the parish church. A few stones remain on the site of Greater Collington church (All Saints) a mile or so to the east.

APPENDIX 1

CROFT (Michael). Blount writes 'Ye church is dedicated to ye Exaltation of ye Holy Crosse', but no other reference appears to support this.

CUSOP (Mary). Local historians claim that the church was founded by and originally dedicated to Cewydd (see p.13), a Radnorshire saint. The parish feast was held on the second Sunday in July (Cewydd's feast day is 2nd July) which has no relevance to the present dedication to Mary. The Domesday form is Cheweshope, and Coplestone Crow writes (BCC pers.) 'The early place-name forms of Cusop do not favour a derivation from Cewydd, though one can see from some of them how it was possible for people to assume that his name was involved.' He and the *DEPN* prefer a Welsh stream-name *Cyw* (*HPN* 63). He continues 'This is not to say that the church was not dedicated to Cewydd: all that can be said is that on present evidence the personal name is not involved in the place-name.'

DEWSALL (Michael). In the 12th century the name appears as *Dewiswelle* (*HPN* 68), and *Foliot* (331 - c.1149) gives *'ecclesiam de Fonte David'*. Since there was a St David's Well it would seem that the church may originally have been dedicated to him.

DORSTONE (Faith). The situation here is very confused. Lewis has Peter, Cassey has Thomas, J & C has Faith, *HCC* 1883 has Mary, while *HCC* 1910 and thereafter give Faith. (See 'Faith' p.18)

EDVIN LOACH (Mary). The old church, now in ruins, was dedicated to St Giles (Egidius)—see *Foliot* 321 (c.1150) *'sancti Egidii de Yeddefen'*. A field near the church is still known as St Giles's Acre. The new church, built c.1860, is dedicated to Mary.

FORD (John of Jerusalem) The present dedication would suggest that the church belonged to the Knights Hospitallers, but documentary evidence indicates that it was in fact a possession of Leominster Priory. It appears that the original dedication—whatever it may have been—lapsed, and in comparatively recent times the dedication to St John of Jerusalem was applied to the church on the mistaken presumption that it had been a dependency of the nearby Preceptory of Dinmore. No dedication is mentioned (it was only a chapelry) until *Kelly* 1895, which has 'dedication uncertain, supposed to be St John of Jerusalem.' No dedication is shown in any *HCC* or *HDY* until 1985, when, and thereafter, John of Jerusalem is given.

FOY (Mary). According to *LL* 275 Bishop Herwald (11th century) dedicated a church at *Lanntiuoi*—Tyvoi or Foy being a disciple of Dyfrig. By the 12th century, owing to a confusion between Tyvoi/Foy and Sainte Foy (St Faith of Agen) the dedication is described as St Faith (*HPN* 86). At some later date, but before 1786, it was changed again to Mary.

GANAREW (Swithin). In 1186 Monmouth Priory had a chapel of St Thomas (probably Becket) here (*CDF* 1129) but this may not have been the parish church, though an inquisition of 1325 mentions 'the church of St Thomas of Ganarew' (*Inquisitiones post mortem* 17E II 75). When the present church was reconsecrated in 1849 after a drastic rebuilding, the bishop accidentally dedicated it to St Luke, and this is given in the 'B stream', but Lewis has Swithin, as do all the *HCC*s and *HDY*s.

HENTLAND (Dubricius). *LL* 275 refers to 'churches of Dyfrig and Teilo in one churchyard' at *Hennlann*.

HOLME LACY (Cuthbert). *Foliot* (321. c.1150) gives '*ecclesiam sancti Cuthberti de Hamma*', and Lewis also gives Cuthbert. The 'B stream' and *HCC* 1883 give Andrew, but J & C and *HCC* 1910 and thereafter give Cuthbert.

HOPE MANSELL (Michael). Before 1160 the village was known as *Hope Ginguene* (*HPN* 105) and Monmouth Priory had the church of St John there (*CDPF* 1145).

HOW CAPLE (Andrew and Mary). Lewis, Cassey and *PO* 1856 give Andrew. *PO* 1863, J & C and *HCC/HDY* until 1969 give Mary. The *HDY* 1970 and thereafter gives Andrew and Mary.

KENDERCHURCH (Mary). Formerly Cynidr (*Llanncinitir, LL* 277). Lewis gives Mary, but *HCC* 1883 gives 'No trace of any saint but Kender - an ancient British saint.' *HCC* 1926 and thereafter give Mary.

KENTCHURCH (Mary). Formerly Keyne/Cein (*Lanncein, LL* 275 and see *HPN* 110).

KILPECK (Mary and David). The parish church was dedicated to David (*LL* 275), and the chapel in the castle to Mary (*Foliot* 302. c.1150) '*ecclesiam sancti David cum capella beate Marie de Kylpec* ...' Presumably when the castle was

APPENDIX 1

demolished the dedication of the chapel was transferred to the church. However Lewis gives David alone, while the 'B stream' give Mary, as does *HCC* 1883. *HCC* 1910 and thereafter give Mary and David.

KING'S PYON (Mary). Coplestone Crow notes (BCC pers.) that the church seems originally to have been dedicated to St Leonard (Dugdale vi 401 viii) and a community of Augustinian Canons established there (*ibid.* 401 ix). In about 1250 the canons moved to Wormsley and set up a priory with a church dedicated to St Leonard. Later the church at King's Pyon was given to Wormsley Priory (*ibid.* 403 xiii). In 1312 *Bishop Swinfield's Register* refers to 'duties to the Virgin Mary in the church at Pyon Regis', so presumably the change in dedication had taken place by then.

LEDBURY (Michael and All Angels). The dedication of Ledbury presents surprising problems. Like Bromyard it was a pre-Conquest minster church, and, like Bromyard, is generally taken to have been dedicated to St Peter throughout the mediaeval period. This is attested by mediaeval documents, *e.g. Hereford Dean and Chapter Muniments* No.1728 (undated, but mid-13th century) and *Bishop Gilbert's Register* p.61 (April 1384). However in the same *Register* for June 1384, in a detailed record of a formal inquisition held by Bishop Gilbert into the status of the churches of Ledbury and Bromyard whether they were collegiate or portionary—we find '*ecclesie beatorum Petri et Pauli de Ledbury et Bromyard.*' No other evidence of the dual dedication at Ledbury is at present forthcoming—though Blount (1675) gives Peter and Paul for Bromyard. But this is not the end, for Ecton (1742) and Bacon (1786) give the dedication as St Michael, and Duncumb (1887) writes 'The church has since been dedicated to St Michael and All Angels.' However directories for the first half of the 19th century all give the dedication as St Peter (*viz.* Pigot 1830 and '35, Hunt 1847, Slater 1850, *PO* 1856, Cassey 1858, Slater 1859 and Morris 1862) whereas *PO* 1863 and all subsequent directories give St Michael and All Angels. A booklet by G. Masefield, *Old Records of Ledbury Church*, published in 1858 gives Peter, but in a reprint of 1895 a MS note adds 'In later years it has been called St Michael.' But the 1871 Census gives Peter.

A possible explanation is that the mediaeval dedication was to St Peter, or SS Peter and Paul, and this continued in popular use until the 1860s. Meanwhile Ecton, following Browne Willis's usual conjecture based on parish feasts, took Ledbury's Michaelmas Fair as indication of a dedication to St Michael. This academic (and mistaken) attribution was generally ignored until 1863, when a controversial rector, the Revd. John Jackson, decided that the

original dedication to St Peter must be discarded in favour of what he took to be the more historically correct one to St Michael and All Angels.
(I am indebted to Joe Hillaby for almost all the references in this section and also for the suggested explanation.)

LEINTHALL STARKES and LEINTWARDINE The present dedication of both these churches is Mary Magdalene, but Blount gives the Blessed Virgin Mary for both.

LEOMINSTER (SS Peter and Paul). For a discussion of early dedications of Leominster Priory see J. Hillaby in *TWNFC* 1987 pp.584-5.

LETTON (John Baptist). Willis gives 'Peter'.

LLANCILLO (Peter). *LL* has '*ecclesiam sancti Sulbiu*' and '*podum Lann Suluiu*' (160). Coplestone-Crow (*HPN* 130) says 'The saint celebrated here is St Tysilio, the premier saint of Powys.' At Sellack Tysilio appears as *Suluc* (*LL* 275-6). Ekwall in *DEPN* points out that '*Suluc* and *Tysilio* are both hypocoristic [*i.e.* familiar] forms of *Suliau*, which was the saint's name.' (see Tysilio, pp.35-6). Mountney (*op.cit* on p.64) queries whether *Sulbiu/Suluiu* at Llancillo is in fact Tysilio, and posits a priest of that name whom Bishop Ufelfyw put in charge of the church there, but it seems doubtful whether the relevant charter (*LL* 160) can bear that interpretation. Blount, Willis and Ecton give no dedication for Llancillo, and from Lewis onwards it is given as Peter.

LLANROTHAL (John Baptist). In *LL* 275 the name is given as *Lannridol*. In *CDF* 1145 as a possession of Monmouth Priory it is given as St Roald. Nothing is known of this saint.

LLANVEYNOE (Beuno and Peter). The original dedication, presumably to its founder Beuno, was lost. Lewis gives Peter, the 'B stream' 'no dedication', *HCC* 1910 and 1926 Michael, but the *HDY* 1960 and thereafter Beuno and Peter.

LLANWARNE (John Baptist). Originally Teilo and Dyfrig (*LL* 275).

LUCTON (Peter). Blount writes 'I find by a very old deed ... the church of St Lawrence in Lucton, but their feast is on the Sunday after 3rd August.' (St Lawrence's feast-day is 10th August.)

APPENDIX 1

LUGWARDINE (Peter). Dugdale in *Monasticon Anglicanum* (Vol. V p.584) prints a charter granted in 1319 by Alan de Plokenet to Abbey Dore including '... the advowson of the church of St Andrew, Lugwardine' (*Andreas de Lugwardyn*).

MADLEY (Nativity of the Blessed Virgin Mary). The dedication was originally perhaps to Ebrdil, mother of Dyfrig (*Inis Ebrdil*, *LL* 79) and then to Dyfrig himself ('*ad Matle ecclesiam Scti Dubricij*', *LL* 194). The present dedication may contain a memory of Ebrdil as a 'Virgin Mother'. In the 14th-century crypt of the parish church there stood a statue of the Blessed Virgin Mary which was an object of pilgrimage, hence the size and splendour of the church.

MARDEN (Mary). Ecton (1742) gives the dedication as Ethelbert, which would be very appropriate for the church built on the site where the saint was first buried. Duncumb however (II. 136) states that Pope Adrian's conditions to Offa for expiation of the murder of Ethelbert were (i) to build a church at Marden and dedicate it to the Blessed Virgin and (ii) to build in stone a church at Hereford, dedicating it to St Ethelbert and translating the saint's body to that church. Unfortunately he gives no reference for this papal decree, but goes on 'The church [at Marden] is mentioned in the *Liber Regis* [Bacon] to be dedicated to St Ethelbert, but the Pope's conditions were not likely to be dispensed with nor does it appear probable that both the cathedral and this church should at the same time and on the same occasion be dedicated to one person.' This argument is hard to follow, for there seems every reason why both cathedral and church should be dedicated to the saint whose death was being expiated. Blount gives 'St Ethelbert King, whose arms are painted on the church wall near the well.' All 19th- and 20th-century directories give Mary, but *Kelly* 1895 refers to the 'church of the Virgin Mary anciently dedicated to St Ethelbert.'

MATHON (John Baptist). *TWNFC* (1951, lxxi) reports the then vicar, the Revd. P.B. Thorburn as saying: 'The church was built by ... Pershore Abbey in 1086... The original dedication was to St Margaret, but at the dissolution of the monasteries the dedication was changed to St John the Baptist.' No evidence for this statement is given.

MONKLAND (All Saints). The 'B stream' give an aberrant dedication to John Baptist, but Lewis has All Saints, as do all other reputable authorities thereafter.

MORDIFORD (Holy Rood). *Foliot* (321. *c*.1150) gives '*ecclesiam sancti Petri de Mordiford*', but there seems to be no other evidence to support this.

OCLE PYCHARD (James the Great). The 'B stream' give an aberrant dedication to Peter, but Lewis has James, as do all other reputable authorities thereafter.

ORLETON (George). Blount gives Nicholas, but this is unsupported.

PRESTON-ON-WYE (Lawrence). Willis gives Peter, but this is unsupported.

ST. DEVEREUX (Dubricius). Blount gives 'Dubritius'; Lewis gives no dedication, nor does *HCC* 1983. *HCC* 1910 and 1926 surprisingly give David (confusion with neighbouring Kilpeck ?), but *HCC* 1940 and thereafter give Dubricius.

SHOBDON (John the Evangelist). According to the *The Anglo-Norman Chronicle of Wigmore Abbey* (J.C. Dickinson and P.T. Ricketts, *TWNFC* xxxix (iii) p.243) in early times there was a wooden chapel of St Juliana at Shobdon. Oliver de Merlimond replaced this with a stone church *c*.1140, and dedicated it to St John the Evangelist.

STAUNTON-ON-ARROW (Peter). Blount gives 'George the Capodocian (sic) Martyr'.

STAUNTON-ON-WYE (Mary). Willis gives Peter and Paul, but this is unsupported.

STOKE EDITH (Mary) Duncumb (IV ii 128) states 'The original church was dedicated to St Edith (daughter of King Edgar), although, as is often found, with the new church the dedication was altered to St Mary.' The church is now dedicated to St Mary and there is no documentary evidence that it was ever dedicated to St Edith, though there is a 'St Edith's well' near the church. What is certain from Domesday is that before the Conquest the manor of Stoke was held by an unspecified Edith; it is probable that this was Queen Edith, wife of Edward the Confessor and sister of King Harold, who was given the title of Saint. There seem therefore to be three possibilities:- (i) that the church was never dedicated to St Edith—but the healing well bears her name, (ii) that Queen Edith dedicated the church to her namesake Edith of Wilton (see p.17),

APPENDIX 1

and (iii) that after the sainted queen's death the church which she had founded was dedicated to her. Blount refers to 'the dedication of the church to St Edytha, but which St Edytha I know not.' (Note: 3 Hen V 1415. *Letters patent. D & C of Hereford* 580 & 586: *'ecclesia beatae Mariae de Stoke Edith'*). Duncumb records that from very early times the parish feast was celebrated on the Sunday following 8th September. Since the feast-day of Edith of Wilton falls on 16th September, he cites this as evidence of an early dedication to her, ignoring the fact that 8th September is the Feast of the Nativity of the Blessed Virgin Mary, pointing rather to an early dedication to St Mary. Lewis and all subsequent 19th- and 20th-century directories give Mary, except *PO* 1863 and *Kelly* 1860, which give Edith.

STOKE LACY (Peter and Paul). Blount writes 'In the church window a picture under written S. Johannes Baptista, yet the Clerk told me the dedication was to St Peter.'

STOKE PRIOR (Luke). Lewis and *PO* 1856 give Michael; Cassey and Slater give Peter; J & C with all *HCC*s give Luke. This dedication was presumably given when the church was rebuilt in 1863.

STRETFORD (Cosmas and Damian). This was the original dedication, and there is in the church a 'shrine' which is said to have held relics of these saints—but see pp.2 & 14. Blount writes 'In the chancel stands a large Case of Stone wherein tradition says were heretofore the Effigies of St Cosmas and Damian ... to whom this church is supposed to be dedicated.' At some time unknown the dedication was changed to St Peter, but in 1920 Cosmas and Damian were reinstated as patrons.

STRETTON GRANDISON (Lawrence). This church belonged to Monmouth Priory, and in 1186 is shown as St Peter (*CDF* 1129). All recent references give Lawrence.

TARRINGTON (Philip and James). Like Stretton Grandison, Tarrington belonged to Monmouth Priory, and likewise in 1186 is shown as St Peter (*CDF* 1129). This too is unsupported by any later sources.

ULLINGSWICK (Luke). No dedication is given in any directory until the *HDD* 1991, so presumably Luke was an invention by the then incumbent. (*PO* 1863 eccentrically suggests 'supposed to have been dedicated in honour of St Helen').

WELLINGTON (Margaret of Antioch). *Foliot* (315. *c*.1150) gives '*ecclesiam beate Margarete de Walinton*'. Willis (1727) and Ecton (1742) give Mary. *Kelly* 1895 gives 'St Margaret, formerly dedicated to St Mary', and all subsequent directories give Margaret. The aberrant Mary presumably springs from Willis.

WELSH BICKNOR (Margaret). It is probable that the original church was dedicated to The Twelve Saints (*Lann idoudecsent*, *LL* 276—and see p.35). There was a church of St Constantine (see p.13) at Hentland in Goodrich (*Lann Custenhinn-garthbenni*, *LL* 276) and this was in the 11th century amalgamated with the church at Welsh Bicknor ('*Lanncusthennin ... Lann Idoudecsent in eodem cimiterio*', *LL* 72). By 1144 Constantine had taken over as patron and the Twelve Saints were forgotten ('*Ecclesiam Scti Custenin de Biconovria*', *CDF* 1142). When Margaret in turn superseded Constantine is not known. Lewis gives Margaret, as do all other 19th- and 20th-century directories except *HCC* 1910 and 1926, which—oddly—give Michael.

WESTON BEGGARD (John Baptist). Willis gives 'Weston-on-Frome, All Saints', but this is unsupported..

WHITCHURCH (Dubricius). According to Coplestone Crow (*HPN* 206) *Lann tiuinauc* in *LL* 275 is Whitchurch, indicating a dedication to St Gwynnog, but by 1325 the dedication is given as Tiburcius, *i.e*. Dubricius/Dyfrig.

WHITNEY-ON-WYE (Peter and Paul). Lewis gives Peter and Paul, but all subsequent directories and the *HCC*s give Paul alone, until *HCC* 1940, which gives Peter and Paul, as do all thereafter.

WINFORTON (Michael and All Angels) See under Cynidr pp.14-5

WOOLHOPE (George). The 'B stream' gives an aberrant dedication to Mary, but Lewis and all subsequent reputable authorities give George.

APPENDIX II

CHARTERS FOR PAROCHIAL FAIRS

I am indebted to Joe Hillaby for the following references to charters granting parochial fairs to be held at the time of a saint's feast-day. It does not follow that the feast-day is that of the church's patron saint, for there may have been local reasons against this, so it is unsafe to argue that any of these charters is evidence, if unsupported, of a mediaeval dedication. On the other hand, they may supply valuable confirmation, as for example in the case of Brampton Bryan. The dedication to St Barnabas, while common in the 19th century, is rare in earlier times, and the fair on St Barnabas's Day at Brampton Bryan demonstrates that this is a genuine mediaeval dedication. The references are as follows:-

C.Ch.R	*Calendar of Charter Rolls* (6 vols. PRO 1903-27)
CR	*Charter Roll Transcripts* (Record Commission, 1837)
IPM	*Inquisitions post mortem* (14 vols. PRO 1904-54)

Bodenham	1378	Assumption of BVM (*C.Ch.R* V,248)
Brampton Bryan	1252	Barnabas (*C.Ch.R* I,377)
Clifford	1261	Assumption of BVM (*C.Ch.R* II,36)
Cradley	1284	Barnabas (*C.Ch.R* II,281)
Fownhope	1221	Mary Magdalene (*CR* I,458)
Huntington (Kington)	1254	Thomas the Martyr (*C.Ch.R* I,192)
Kilpeck	1309	Assumption of BVM (*C.Ch.R* III,127)
Kingsland	1306	Michael (*C.Ch.R* III,68)

Kinnersley	1357	James (*C.Ch.R* V,155)
Lea	1343	Invention of the Cross (*C.Ch.R* V,24)
	1347	Bartholomew (*C.Ch.R* V,70)
Leominster	1189	Peter and Paul (*Reading Abbey Cartularies* ed. B.R. Kemp (1986) I,61)
Lyonshall	1227	Simon & Jude (*C.Ch.R* I,43)
	1301 & 1319	Michael (*C.Ch.R* III, 1 & 414)
Madley	1202	Nativity of BVM (*C.Ch.R* III,212-3)
Moccas	1328	John Baptist (*C.Ch.R* IV.90)
Much Cowarne	1255	Michael (*C.Ch.R* I,447)
Preston-on-Wye	1253	Lawrence (*C.Ch.R* I,435)
Staunton-on-Wye	1294	George (*C.Ch.R* II,436)
Thruxton	1294	Leonard (*C.Ch.R* II,454) (subsequently disallowed II,471)
Wigmore	1304	James (*IPM* IV,157-235)
Winforton	1318(2)	James, and Crispin & Crispinian (*C.Ch.R* III,409)

APPENDIX III

INABWY / JUNABIUS

Inabwy presents several problems. In the Book of Llandaff the name appears twelve times, spelt variously Iunabui, Iunapius and Iunapeius, mostly in charters which Wendy Davies dates between 575 and 620.

The first entry (*LL* 72) concerns the grant of land at Garthbenni (see also Welsh Bicknor p.58 and *HPN* p.33) by King Peipiau '*deo et Dubricio archiepiscopo sedis Llandavie et Iunapeio consobrino suo.*' Since Peipiau is the subject of the sentence, this should mean that Inabwy was Peipiau's cousin, but it seems more likely that he was Dyfrig's, since Peipiau (according to the *Vita* in *LL*) was Dyfrig's grandfather. Iunapeius appears as a clerical witness to this charter.

In the latest charters (*LL* 163b and 164) in which Inabwy appears we find '*Iunapeius episcopus*'. Davies (*LC* p.177) writes: 'It is possible that Iunabui is a different person from Iunapeius, but perhaps more likely that the names, since they are rare, represent the same man.' The charters are arranged in what is intended to be chronological order, grouped under the names of the successive bishops in office. *LL* 163 and 164 are under the heading of '*Iunapeius Episcopus*'. The historically suspect lists of bishops in *LL* 303 and 311 purport to show a chronological succession of single bishops, thus validating the antiquity of the see of Llandaff and the succession from Dyfrig. While Dyfrig, who is sometimes described as '*archiepiscopus*', and possibly Teilo also, may have had episcopal authority over most of south-east Wales, in the later 6th century it seems that there were local bishops in Gwent, Glamorgan and Archenfield (Ergyng), so that some of the early names in the episcopal lists in *LL* will have held office concurrently rather than consecutively. The seventh name on the lists is '*Lunapeius*': the headings of the charters confirm that this is an error for

Iunapeius, and it can be assumed that Inabwy was Bishop in Ergyng rather than of Llandaff.

The final problem associated with Inabwy arises from a charter (*LL 73a*) dated *c*.585 by which King Peipiau gives *podum Iunabui* to Dyfrig and his successors in the see of Llandaff, with *Iunabui presbiter* as one of the witnesses. Davies (*LC* p.93) identifies this *podum* with Llandinabo, but Evans (*LL* p.364) points out that the boundaries set out in the charter refer to the River Guy (Wye), and while Llandinabo is two miles from the Wye, the boundaries will fit well for Bredwardine—and Coplestone Crow agrees (*HPN* p.42). Furthermore, in a list of churches in Ergyng in *LL* 275 we find '*Lann hunapui*' (sic) coming between Peterstow and Llanwarne. This is obviously Llandinabo. It seems unlikely that Hunapui and Iunabui are the same person for, as has been pointed out, Iunabui appears frequently in *LL* as priest and bishop, and is spelt Iunabui, Iunapui and Iunapeius, but never Hunabui. Was Llandinabo then dedicated to the otherwise unknown Hunapui (as Coplestone Crow suggests, *HPN* p.131) and later assimilated to the better-known Iunabui/Inabwy?

References to Appendices

In these references, the following notation is used. The full details of the sources referred to can be found in the Bibliography.

BCC (pers)	B. Coplestone Crow - personal communication
CDF	J.H. Round (ed.) - *Calendar of documents preserved in France*
DEPN	E. Ekwall - *Concise Oxford Dictionary of English Place-names*
Foliot	*The Letters and Charters of Gilbert Foliot*
HPN	B. Coplestone Crow - *Herefordshire Place-names*
LC	Wendy Davies - *The Llandaff Charters*
LL	*The Text of the Book of Llan Dav* ed. Evans and Rhys
Rees	W. Rees - *Map of South Wales and the Border in the 14th Century* (1933)
TWNFC	Transactions of the Woolhope Naturalists' Field Club

DIRECTORIES
HCC	*Church Calendar and Clergy List of the Diocese of Hereford*
HDY	*Hereford Diocesan Year-book*
HDD	*Hereford Diocesan Directory*

These are the successive titles of the annual diocesan directory. For the secular directories—Cassey, Jakeman & Carver, Kelly, Lewis, Post Office and Slater—see the Bibliography.

Bibliography

Arnold-Foster, F. *Studies in Church Dedications* (Skeffington 1899)
Bacon, John *Liber Regis vel Thesaurus Rerum Ecclesiasticarum* (London 1786)
Blount, Thomas *The 1675 Thomas Blount MS History of Herefordshire* Transcribed and researched by Richard and Catherine Botzum. Translation and editing: Norman C. Reeves (Hereford n.d. Lapridge Publications)
Bond, Francis *Dedications and Patron Saints of English Churches* (O.U.P. 1914)
Butler, A. ed. Thurston & Attwater *Lives of the Saints* (Burns, Oates & Washbourne 1936)
Cassey, Edward & Co. *History, Topography & Directory of Herefordshire* (1858)
Church Calendar and Clergy List of the Diocese of Hereford (annual directory)
Coplestone Crow, B. *Herefordshire Place-names* (1989)
Davies, Wendy *The Llandaff Charters* (1977)
Doble, G.H. ed. D.S. Evans *Lives of the Welsh Saints* (U.W.P. 1993)
Dickinson, J.C. and P.T. Ricketts *TWNFC* xxxix (111) p.243
Dugdale, W. *Monasticon Anglicanum*, ed. Caley, Ellis & Bandinel (London 1817-30)
Duncumb. J. and continuators *Collections towards the History and Antiquities of the County of Hereford* (1804-1915)
Ecton, John *Thesaurus Rerum Ecclesiasticarum* (2nd ed. London 1754)
Ekwall, E. *Concise Oxford Dictionary of English Place-names* (Oxford 1960)
Evans, J.G. and J. Rhys (eds.) *The Text of the Book of Llan Dav* (1893) (References are given to the pages of this edition.)
Farmer, D.H. *The Oxford Dictionary of Saints* (2nd ed. O.U.P. 1979)
Foliot, Gilbert *The Letters and Charters of Gilbert Foliot*, ed. Morby & Brooke (C.U.P. 1967) (References are given to the charters as numbered in this edition.)
Hereford Diocesan Directory (annual)
Hereford Diocesan Year-book (later *Hereford Diocesan Directory*)
Heys, F.G. *TWNFC*, 1960 p.343-
Jakeman & Carver, *Directory and Gazetteer of Herefordshire* (Hereford 1870)

Kelly's Directory (annual directory)

Lewis, Samuel *Topographical Dictionary of England* (4 vols. 1st ed. 1831: 5th ed. 1842)

Mountney, M. *The Saints of Herefordshire* (Express Logic, Hereford 1976)

Orme, Nicholas *English Church Dedications—with a Survey of Cornwall and Devon* (University of Exeter Press 1996)

Martin, S.H. *TWNFC*, 1934, p.219-

Post Office Directory (annual directory)

Rees, W. *Map of South Wales and the Border in the 14th Century* (1933)

Round. J.H. (ed), *Calendar of documents preserved in France* (London 1899)

Slater *Slater's Royal National & Commercial Directory & Topography* (1859)

Willis, Browne *Survey of Cathedrals* (1727-1730)

Directories

From about 1830 onwards a proliferation of national and county directories appeared, many of them purporting to give the dedications of parish churches. It might be expected that these would be a useful source of information, but unfortunately many of them are patently unreliable on this topic, and the compilers uncritically copied the mistakes of their predecessors. For Herefordshire the most reliable lineage (A) runs from Samuel Lewis's *Topographical Dictionary of England* (1831) through Jakeman & Carver's *Dictionary and Gazetteer of Herefordshire* (1890). Another stream (B)— patently unreliable as far as dedications are concerned—runs from Edward Cassey's *History, Topography and Directory of Herefordshire* (1858), through Slater (1859) and the Post Office Directories of 1856 and 1863, to the first appearance of Kelly in 1870. As examples of this confusion one may quote Dorstone, which is given as Peter (Lewis), Thomas (*PO* 1856 and Cassey), Mary (*PO* 1863 and Kelly 1870) and Faith (Jakeman 1890), or Weobley, where all the 'B stream' give Mary, while the 'A stream' correctly give Peter and Paul. In view of the unreliability of the 'B stream' these have not usually been quoted as references, while Lewis is a valuable witness, being both early and scholarly, and Jakeman & Carver, a local publisher who seem to have used Lewis, are also trustworthy. The later editions of Kelly are largely free from the inherited errors of the earlier editions, and are therefore useful.

As for diocesan directories, the *Church Calendar and Clergy List of the Diocese of Hereford* includes no dedications until 1853; from then onwards it is presumably authoritative. In 1954 this publication became *The Hereford Diocesan Year-book* and it is now *The Hereford Diocesan Directory*.